English
FOR YOUR
Success

**A Language Development Program
for African American Children
Grades Pre-K-8**

**A Handbook of Successful Strategies
for Educators**

Los Angeles Unified School District
and Noma LeMoine

Peoples Publishing Group, Inc.

Free to Learn, to Grow, to Change

Credits:

Project Manager, Doreen Smith

Editor, Randy Ross, Ph.d.

Copy Editor, Christine Cannistraro

Cover Design, Jeremy Mayes

Design, Jeremy Mayes, Doreen Smith, Brooke Kaska

Production/Electronic Design, Doreen Smith, Brooke Kaska

Photo Credits:

Cover Illustrations by Doris Hughes

Interior photos provided by Noma Lemoine

ISBN 1-56256-440-4

© 1999

The Peoples Publishing Group
299 Market Street
Saddle Brook, New Jersey 07663

Printed in the United States of America
10   9   8   7   6   5   4

ACKNOWLEDGEMENTS

SIDNEY A. THOMPSON, SUPERINTENDENT OF SCHOOLS
LOS ANGELES UNIFIED SCHOOL DISTRICT

JESSIE G. FRANCO, ASSISTANT SUPERINTENDENT, LANGUAGE
ACQUISTION/BILINGUAL DEVELOPMENT BRANCH

NOMA LEMOINE, DIRECTOR, LANGUAGE DEVELOPMENT PROGRAM FOR
(principal writer)   AFRICAN AMERICAN STUDENTS

STRATEGIES HANDBOOK DEVELOPMENT COMMITTEE

NOMA LEMOINE, CHAIRPERSON

PAMELA BLANKS	SUBIRA KIFANO	MICHAEL HAGGOOD	JEAN ROLLINS
ANTHONY JACKSON	PAMELA GATES	GAIL J. QUARLES	SHARROKY HOLLIE
ROSALYN DEGRAFFINREID	CHRISTOPHER MOGGIA	MIRIAM HOOPER	SUNDREYA SMITH

Teacher Handbook Lesson Development Group

Amy Ahlfeld
Anita Allen
Diane Allen
William Alexander
Anne Apakama
Lynn Barat
Shirley Bass
Bertha Beasley
Robbie Belcher
Kim Hurley-Bell
Rose Bennett
Grace Bishop
Jeanne Blessings
Jack Bommarito
Roberta Hagen-Brandt
Robin Brewington
Jacqueline Brown
Joanne Brown
Dr. Merrick Brown
Nadine Brown
Susan Van-Buren
Corean Burns
Louise Burns
Stephanie Burrus
Cynthia Calhoun
Artis Callahan
Thomas Campbell
Patricia Carey
Betty Carson
Carl Carson
Kathleen Carter
Shirley Chapman
Cynthia Coleman
Janet Collins
Lisa Collins
Tanya Cotton
Gloria Crawford
Starletta Darbeau
Kimberly Davis

Cynthia Dawkins
Kathryn Dawson
Betty Joseph Dearth
Michelle Delandy
Chrystal Battey-Dorsey
Angela Dotson
Vanessa Dotson
Betty Douglas
Lori Eldeman
Terry Elloitt
Sharon Elston
James English
Betty Esters
Elizabeth Fields
Evelyn Finley
Celeste Fobia
Gayle Forbes
Bettye Foreman
Mary Fothergill
Augusto Francisco
Mary Fringinal
Irma Fuller
Dorothy Gardner
Andriette Gibson
Vivian Gillum
Marcia Gillyard
Carolyn Givens
LaVerna Govan
Barbara Grant
Pamela Green
Minnie Hadley
Sta-C Hale
Kenneth Harris
Norma Harris
Beatrice Harrison
Evelyn Hearn
Kyla Hinson
Fay Hockaday
Barbara Holligan

Brenda Howard
Deborah Jackson
Kery Jackson
Martha Jaminez
Dana Humphrey-Johnson
Rachel Johnson
Rosa Jones
Thea Taylor-Jones
Karen Joseph
Pamela Joseph
Jennifer King
Frances Leon
A. Kay Smith-Lewis
Bonnie Lewis
Gloria Livas
Kimberly Lovelace
E. Anne Lyles
Helmtrud Magee
Donald Mahoney
Stephen Malone
Angela Manuel
Alex Martin
Beverly Martin
Urusla Martin
Janelle Mault
Cassandra May
Cheri McDonald
Nalis Mercier
John Merrill
Stephanie Miles
Laura Minkin
Ella Morrison
Mary Ann Moss
Ameerah Abdul Mujeeb
Nikki Ndubuisi
Nailah Nicolas
James Norman
Tanya Norrell

Lisa O'Brian
Lyn-Felice Ollie
Allison O'Quinn
Shelia Orange
Lovette Osborne
Vera Parker
Shirley Perkins
Elise Posey
Merry Pickett
Georgia Powell
Daisy Redic
Geraldine Reese
Eleanor Richard
Zelendria Robinson
Melinda Rodriquez
Cindy Rodgers
Janelle Rogers
Elsie Roper
Hawaii Cannon-Ross
Marsha Ross
Marsha Rowe
Daniel Russell
Nancy Russell
Shelia Salley
Thelma Samuel
Margaret Sarrell
Andrea Adams-Scott
Dean Seislove
Ioanna Sklaveniti
Deborah Smith
Diane Smith
Erika Smith
Jeryl Smith
Kaye Smith
Jacqueline Snead
Clara Sparks
Dorie Spencer
Charlene Stewart
Patricia Schwartz

Patricia Swiderski
Dawna Stinson
Tanya Stokes
Kevin Sved
LaVivian Taylor
Nadine Brown-Taylor
Evelyn Finley-Taylor
Nina Kirby-Taylor
Dean Thornbald
Aurora Frank-Thompson
Eudora Thurman
Simone Smith- Tiger
Arie Udeze
Pauletta Varnado
Adrian Villasenor
Eleanor Walker
Myrna Walker
Kemala Washington
LeShun Washington
Sylvia Washington
Carol Alson-Watson
Calpurina Weathersby
Jeanne Weinberg
Jacqueline Wheeler
Susan Whitsell
Gloria Wilkerson
Arlene Williams
Barbara Williams
Bernita Williams
Carolyn Williams
Darryl Williams
Lynn Williams
Sharon Wilson
Renita Woods
Rose Wooten

Contents

🟰 Noma LeMoine

CHAPTER 1

INTRODUCTION

One day years ago while working as a speech/language pathologist for the Los Angeles Unified School District, I was sitting in a school office waiting to be escorted to a classroom. A teacher entered with an African American child. It appeared the teacher wanted to telephone the child's parents. The teacher looked up at the student and said, "Bobby, what does your mother do everyday?"

"She *be* at home!" Bobby said.

"You mean, she *is* at home," the teacher corrected.

"No, she ain't," Bobby said, "'cause she took my grandmother to the hospital this morning."

"You know what I meant," the teacher said. "You are not supposed to say, 'she *be* at home.' You are to say, 'she *is* at home.'"

"Why you trying to make me lie?" Bobby said. "She ain't at home."

The scene escalated and the disgruntled teacher eventually escorted Bobby to the principal's office.

This episode illustrates the problem of trying to correct African American Language (AAL) into Mainstream American English (MAE). Bobby's teacher had attempted to collapse an African linguistic structure into an English structure. This is tantamount to correcting French into English. It cannot happen. The confusion derives from the common vocabulary of the two languages. African American Language has an English vocabulary and lexicon, and teachers tend to believe that many African American children speak a corrupt or incorrect form of English. Knowledge of the system of rules governing AAL would help to disabuse teachers of this false notion. A teacher with this understanding would not attempt to "correct" this language form. Rather, the teacher would teach the new set of rules which govern the new language form.

When the teacher said, "She is at home," Bobby became confused linguistically. He interpreted this to mean that his mother was at home at the moment, which was not true. When Bobby said, "She be at home," he meant that it is her habit to be home on a day-to-day basis.

This example shows how communication can backfire when a child lacks understanding of the structure of MAE and the teacher has no understanding of the structure of AAL. While the well-meaning teacher took advantage of a teachable grammar moment, unfortunately her instruction relied on a faulty interpretation of Bobby's language.

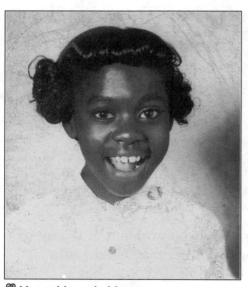
❀ Young Noma LeMoine

I, too, have experienced this type of denigration. Having attended segregated schools in Austin, Texas, I moved with my family to Los Angeles when I was in junior high school. Initially, I found myself in an inner-city Los Angeles school whose enrollment was virtually all African American. However, unlike my Austin school, the teachers were not all African American. Through my new experience with non-African American teachers, I soon discovered how it feels to have your cognitive ability judged on the basis of your proficiency in MAE. I discovered how it felt to be made to feel stupid because I spoke AAL.

But, in my case, I was fortunate to be the youngest child of a father who possessed an unflagging belief in the capacity of his eleven children.

"You're a Bunton," he would always say. "All my kids are geniuses. And if anybody tells you different, they're a liar."

The strong support from my father, mother, and older siblings helped me to overcome the perhaps unintended efforts of those teachers to dent my self-esteem. I was a Bunton. I would pursue excellence in everything I did, no matter what anyone said to the contrary.

Many African American children undergo similar educational experiences bereft of the staunch familial support that I enjoyed. Teachers perceive that these children suffer a language deficiency when, in fact, they have mastered the language of the home and arrive at school ready to learn. As educators we expect students to employ and expand their knowledge of the language of instruction, but we do not know how to facilitate this learning. As a result, educational institutions have failed many African American children.

In hindsight, my decision to become a speech and language pathologist can be traced back to my early experiences as a student in the inner-city public schools of Los Angeles. If many teachers viewed my language as an inadequate representation of MAE, then the Bunton creed demanded that I master MAE. At the same time, I remained attached to the language of my home. My parents, siblings, and I so naturally and effortlessly used a different language from that which was used in Los Angeles schools. Our language was rich and rhythmical and full of color. Thus, in effect, I became bilingual. Becoming a language specialist was a natural progression for me. Indeed, I discovered later that one of my sisters had also studied to become a speech pathologist. It figures-she was just a couple of years older than me and had no doubt been subjected to similar disparaging treatment in her introduction to Los Angeles schools.

While working for several years as a speech and language pathologist for Los Angeles Unified, I began to review research on the language of African Americans. This research presented evidence that the language of African Americans is a unique language that has a clearly definable structure and system of rules. If this finding were valid, it meant that many language-different black children were being deprived of a quality education: this is because most of their teachers neither acknowledged nor understood the language of these children. Indeed, the numerical over-representation of African American children in special education could be explained in part by this shortcoming of many teachers. That is, many so-called speech or language impediments are actually language differences which should result in placement in English as a Second Language (ESL)—not placement in special education.

Eventually I became a speech and language diagnostic specialist. During this period, I began building a knowledge base in language variation in African American children. Subsequently, while working as a special education teacher, it became clear that many of my African American students had been misdiagnosed as communication-impaired, when in fact

❊ Working as a speech & language diagnostic specialist, I realized many African American students employed a different language than that taught at school—AAL.

they employed a different language form—the language of their homes, or AAL. I wondered, too, what was happening to similar children in regular classrooms. Were their language needs understood? Or was their home language waylaid by the acerbic words of their teachers?

In 1989, while I was serving as the Coordinating Administrator of the Los Angeles Unified School District's (LAUSD) speeech and language program, the District published the report, "The Children Can No Longer Wait." This report corroborated my new-found understanding of the language of African American children. In the report, the Los Angeles Unified School District acknowledged that many African American children and their families speak a language (AAL) that differs structurally from MAE. Indeed, AAL has its own system of rules, sounds, and meaning. The report concluded that this language should be recognized and valued, just as any other foreign language. The report recommended that a program be created that would teach standard English as a second language to speakers of nonstandard English.

When LAUSD sought a director for the new program, I immediately applied. When the District's advisory group selected me to direct the program, I was deeply honored and eager to develop and implement the program.

This is the resulting program, *English for Your Success,* also referred to as the Language Development Program for African American Students (LDPAAS). It is a research-based program which uses a second-language acquisition model that emphasizes communication through content, enhances the development of academic language, and assures literacy. English for Your Success:

❧ requires instruction on ancient Africa, its cultures, history, and impact on the contemporary world—includes the history of African Americans with emphasis on African American achievers, both historical and contemporary;

❧ stresses logical and critical thinking skills through problem solving across the content areas; and

❧ uses teaching strategies that capitalize on identified student strengths.

What is different about this program is that it validates the home language of many African American students. The view that AAL is definably distinct places a formidable pressure on many educators to change how they view language, how they view culture, and indeed how they view individuals who speak AAL.

This handbook describes the instructional approaches EYS has introduced to Los Angeles to help teachers improve the quality of language instruction provided to African American students. However, teachers will adopt these approaches only when they believe that the culture—including the language spoken by most African American children and their parents—is valid and worthy of respect in the classroom.

Dr. Wade Nobles once noted that culture is to humans as water is to fish—the two defy separation. Yet to place salt water fish in fresh water would subject them to extreme trauma. Similarly, placing African American children in a mainstream educational environment could foment stress in those students. This is because the students have been placed in an unfamiliar culture in which they are expected to perform as they would in their native environment. As Dr. Nobles notes, remedies exist for this salty problem: we could return the salt water fish to their natural habitat, or if this were not practical, we could add salt to the fresh water.

In a sense, this book discusses ways of putting a little salt into the education of African American students by adopting culturally appropriate curriculum and education practices. As teachers, we need to ensure that what occurs in our classrooms builds upon what children bring to school behaviorally, linguistically, and experientially.

First, we briefly review how children learn language. Second, we trace the emergence of our view that African Americans employ a distinct, rule-based language that has its origins in the languages of West Africa. The primary purpose of this discussion is to assist educators in tossing off the widespread habit of viewing the language of African Americans as a deficient offshoot of MAE. Next, we describe instructional goals and strategies that support these children in their acquisition of MAE.

※ The development of language in children is not innate; children learn the language of the home they are reared in.

Chapter 2

Normal Language Development in Children

People seem to have an innate ability to develop oral or spoken language. Indeed, children become fluent in language between infancy and the age of four. During their first four years of life, children subconsciously intuit the rules of the language of the home. This behavior is not ethnic specific. For example, an African American infant placed with surrogate parents in Japan will become fluent in Japanese. Children learn the language in which they are immersed.

The first four years in life are critical for language acquisition. Between infancy and four years, youngsters begin to perceive the rules that underlie the communication of the model in their home. Moreover, contrary to the traditional view, children do not achieve language fluency by imitating the sounds made by their parents. Children generate their own language form as they perceive the underlying rules of this form.

By two months of age, infants begin to link consonant and vowel sounds. Some theorists maintain that crying is actually the beginning of language acquisition. Children play with sounds early. They begin to babble. Even deaf children, who babble as well, begin linking consonant and vowel sounds together, as would be done by children with normal hearing.

By 6 to 8 months of age, the environment becomes a critical variable in the continuation of the language acquisition process. We know this because at this point, deaf children cease to babble or make sounds. Hearing children expand their sound production to incorporate inflections and intonations with the rhythm or prosodic elements of the language of the home. A child in a home where Japanese is spoken begins to sound Japanese. If the language of the home is Spanish, then the child begins to sound Spanish.

By 6 to 8 months of age . . . children . . . incorporate inflections and intonations with the rhythm or prosodic elements of the language of the home.

Languages have distinctive patterns, as reflected, for example, by differences in rhythm and inflection. These patterns often enable us to decipher the ethnicity of a person on the phone, whether we see the person or not. This cultural phenomenon occurs as early as 6 to 8 months of age.

Between the ages of two and three, the child senses how to order words in a meaningful way (syntax). Two and three words are strung together. The child might say, "See Daddy shoe," or "Mommy, go store." These language structures represent the child's early attempts to master the language of the home.

The child turns three and experiences a surge in morphological development. Past tense, plurals, noun and verb agreement become part of the child's linguistic repertoire. Children hear *ed* added to make the past tense, and they pick it up. "Mommy cook-ed, Mommy look-ed." Initially, they over-generalize the rule. They also learn more about irregular past tense forms. When they say "go-*ed*" - they hear Mommy say, "We *went* yesterday." Children constantly pick up language elements, process them, and place them in context, until, by age four, they have mastered the language of the home.

. . . by age four [children] have mastered the language of the home.

※ Some researchers attest that African Americans face a anatomical "deficit" preventing the articulation of the English language.

CHAPTER 3

HISTORICAL DEVELOPMENT OF AFRICAN AMERICAN LANGUAGE

While the language of African Americans can be readily distinguished from mainstream English, history has offered provocative explanations as to why the difference exists. Research journals from 1820s advanced a "deficit" perspective which purported that Africans in America could not employ American English primarily because: (1) they lacked the cognitive ability to learn a new language; and (2) they were anatomically or physiologically deviant, their tongues too thick and their lips too full to articulate the "fine" sounds of the English language.[1] While this "deficit" perspective does not match the linguistic reality of Africans, unfortunately it continues to color the thinking of many educators.[2]

Confronted with mounting evidence against the deficit theory, some 19th century researchers began to say that African Americans speak a dialect of the English language. That is, their language has the same rules as English but manifests some surface structure variations as, for example, in the accent of a Bostonian or New Yorker.[3] This "black dialect" perspective represented the beginning of an attempt to acknowledge that enslaved Africans brought language with them which may have influenced how African Americans speak.

English speaking slavers (including Americans) arriving on the West Coast of Africa could not speak African languages. Creolists noted that a simplified trade language or "pidgin" developed, which borrowed from English and the Bantu languages [Gullah].

Neither the "deficit" nor "black dialect" perspectives on the language of African Americans requires an understanding of the languages of the peoples of Africa. Creolist researchers connected African languages to the language of Africans in America. The Creolists' theory traces African American Language to the beginnings of the Slave Trade. English speaking slavers (including Americans) arriving on the West Coast of Africa could not speak African languages. Creolists noted that a simplified trade language or *pidgin* developed, which borrowed from English and the Bantu languages. This trade language enabled communication between the English speaking slavers and Africans. Furthermore, the Creolists note that this *pidgin* was spoken by many of the enslaved Africans who were separated from their indigenous languages. The Creolists speculated that this pidgin developed into its own language form (Gullah), which the Creolists view as the origin of "Black English."[4]

Another group of researchers, the Ethnolinguists, disagrees with all of the theories discussed above. Their theory considers the deficit perspective racist, having no basis in the linguistic history of Africans. It rejects the view that AAL is a dialect of English. Ethnolinguists argue that the "deep" structure of the language of enslaved Africans in America is governed more by Niger-Congo or Bantu rules than English rules. Ethnolinguists also find the Creolist hypothesis incredible in its reliance on the premise that millions of Africans brought here for enslavement relied on a trade *pidgin* for communication. Enslaved Africans spoke indigenous African languages; if they did speak *pidgin*, it was their second, third or fourth language form.[5]

Ethnolinguists define AAL as a continuation of African languages in America.[6] Africans came to this country as speakers of indigenous Bantu languages. The conditions of slavery forced them to learn English vocabulary, which they

Africans came to this country as speakers of indigenous Bantu languages. The conditions of slavery forced them to learn English vocabulary, which they subconsciously integrated into the structure of their indigenous Bantu language. Anyone acquiring a second language goes through a similar process.

subconsciously integrated into the structure of their indigenous Bantu language. Anyone acquiring a second language goes through a similar process.

The Ethnolinguistic theory invokes the sordid history of the African slave trade. Africans were transported under inhuman conditions, chained together in hulls of ships for months on the ocean. Indeed, conditions aboard slave ships were so wretched that often when enchained Africans were taken to the deck for air, they would throw themselves overboard. Historians estimate that the remains of six to 12 million Africans lay on the floor of the Atlantic Ocean.[7]

Massive losses of their human cargo led slavers to separate the Africans into different language groups in order to hamper communication. The slavers reasoned that linguistically diverse ethnic groups would be less able to make quick joint decisions to jump overboard. This strategy extended to America's slave auction blocks. Plantation owners caught on that purchasing six Yoruba was unwise. It was better to mix and mingle the Africans.

Thus began the breakup of the Black family—mother and child were separated and sold to different plantation owners to break down communication. Africans on plantations could not use their indigenous African languages partly because they were separated from their own groups and partly because they were restricted from covening in groups larger than two or three. Furthermore, Southern states instituted laws that promised death for Africans caught using African language in America.

These restrictions affected the development of African American Language. There are two ways to learn language: intuitively by subconsciously divining the rules of the language from their primary caregivers or formally in school. Enslaved Africans did

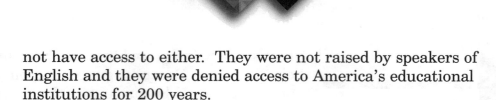

not have access to either. They were not raised by speakers of English and they were denied access to America's educational institutions for 200 years.

Noting that their forebears came to America and learned American English, many European Americans wonder why Africans did not also master the language more readily. It seems incomprehensible to them that Africans should not have been able to do so.

However, the historical experiences of Africans and other groups in America differ in important ways. When Europeans flooded America's shores in the early 20th century, they came seeking freedom, opportunity, jobs, and religious freedom. They were not the elite of Europe: many lacked education. It is important to note, however, that Europeans inherited the right to vote. One thing they voted for was public education. As a result, their children entered American schools and learned the language of their new country.

By contrast, enslaved Africans in the South were denied access to formal education for over 200 years. Africans also did not have political rights. The Voting Rights Act, enacted in August 1965, is barely 30 years old.

The third variable was economics. Many European families were able to put money aside for the first time and send their children to college. Enslaved Africans worked but received no pay and their children had access to neither primary schools nor colleges.

In short, relative to others who have clambered to America's shores, Africans were deprived of political, economic, and educational opportunities. Despite these inequities, African people developed their language form without the benefit of educational institutions.

[1] See, for example, Bareiter and Englemann (1966) and Bernstein (1951).

[2] See, for example, Spache (1975).

[3] See Fasold abd Shuy (1970), Labov (1970), Stewart (1968), and Wolfram (1969).

[4] See Bailey (1966), Dillard (1972), Smitherman (1977), Stewart (1967), and Turner (1949).

[5] See Alleyne (1971), Smith (1977), Welmers (1977).

[6] See Williams (1970).

[7] See Jackson (1996), pp. 44-45 (provides 1.5 to 2million).

✥ AAL has it origins in languages of Africa. Teachers must learn the key features of these languages to better understand AAL.

CHAPTER 4

CHARACTERISTIC LINGUISTIC FEATURES OF AFRICAN AMERICAN LANGUAGE

Teachers who work with African American children probably recognize the distinctive features of the language these children speak. However, it is important for teachers to grasp that these features have their origin in the languages of Africa. To help fill this void in teachers' knowledge and understanding of AAL, in this section we relate key features of this language to their African origin.

Ethnolinguists have traced the sound distinctions in Ebonics (including AAL) to the Niger-Congo or Bantu language system. Alleyne has noted, for example, that the *th* sound is almost non-existent in the phonological system of Niger-Congo.[8] As a result, speakers of AAL generally do not employ this sound when they speak. When an African American child says, "Dey don't know what dey talkin' about," do we view this child as coming from a linguistic background that does not recognize the *th* sound and that, therefore, the child is employing a phonemic approximation? Similarly, the English *er* sound is not among the collection of sounds in Niger-Congo. In AAL sister becomes sis*tah*. The same is true of the *l* sound located in the middle of words. Speakers of AAL will say, "I wish I could win a *mi(l)yon* (million) dollars." These phonological variations derive from the Bantu system.

Note that the *th* sound does not exist in French either. Native French speakers learning English as a second language say *d*is, *d*en, *d*ese, and *d*ose, just as African Americans say *d*is, *d*en, *d*ese, and *d*ose. For the French, this phonetic approximation is

. . . the *th* sound does not exist in French either. Native French speakers learning English as a second language say *dis, den, dese,* and *dose,* just as African Americans do.

considered an accent. When African Americans employ this approximation, teachers often view it as an educational deficit. Teachers, in effect, tell African American kids they are speaking incorrectly. This is a bias in American culture that the ethnolinguistic perspective begins to correct. African Americans are endowed with knowledge of an indigenous rule system against which they lay an English vocabulary system. Once teachers recognize that AAL is Bantu-rich rather than English-deficient, we will have a better basis for helping these children master the language of instruction.

In the Bantu system, consonant clusters do not exist when they have the same voicing and occur at the end of words. The Bantu word pattern typically alternates consonants and vowels—a

. . . AAL is Bantu-rich rather than English-deficient . . .

consonant is almost always followed by a vowel sound. When this pattern does not occur, the Bantu rule requires the insertion of a vowel or the deletion of a consonant.[9] For example, speakers of AAL pronounce *desk* as *des* and *test* as *tes*. An African American child might say, "I put my *tes* on your *des*."

The consonant cluster feature affects the language in a variety of ways, not only in word patterning. The corrective approach would entail re-teaching all the words in English. That is not how language is learned. Language is learned through the rules which govern it. Thus, children need to acquire knowledge of the rules, not the forms.

An interesting outcome of this consonant cluster difference is that we end up with many homophones (words that sound alike but that have different meanings) such as *find* and *fine* which do not exist in Mainstream American English. They become homophones for speakers of AAL. Knowledge of these words aids educators in teaching speakers of AAL to read.[10]

Past tense forms with two unvoiced consonant sounds at the end do not exist in the Bantu language structure

Some consonant clusters affect how African American children pronounce past tense forms. Words with two unvoiced consonant sounds at the end are rare in the Bantu language structure, so many African American children sound out "Bobby *kicked* me" as "Bobby *kick* me."

Grammatical rules in the Bantu system of language also help to explain the language of African American students. For example, while MAE uses the letter *s* as a possessive marker, the *s* is not needed to demonstrate possession in Niger-Congo or Bantu. When African American children say, "That *John* cousin," or "That *Betty* book," American teachers are apt to send them to a speech pathologist. However, a deeper understanding of AAL counters the notion that these children cannot produce the possessive *s* sound because their tongues are too thick. These children can produce the possessive *s* sound, but because the Bantu system of language does not require the *s* to denote possession, the *s* sound is not produced in this context. Thus the statement, "That *John* cousin," demonstrates possession within the Bantu system by placing stress or emphasis on the posssessor. The Chinese language also does not use *s* as a possessive marker. Again, different languages have different rules.

. . . the *s* is not needed to demonstrate possession in Niger Congo or Bantu . . . Chinese, among other Asian languages, also does not use *s* as a possessive marker

The *s* does serve as a plural marker in the Bantu system, but it is seldom used in conjunction with a number word or numerical quantifier. Thus, Bantu rules would prompt a speaker of AAL to say "I have five *cent*" instead of "I have five *cents*." This is appropriate because the numerical quantifier identifies the number. In Bantu, it would be redundant to add an *s* to *cent*. Again, African American children can produce the *s* sound, but their root language prohibits the production of this sound in certain contexts.

Similar differences occur with noun-verb agreement. The Bantu system, like most languages, has a regular verb system. In Spanish, for example, verbs can be memorized easily because few exceptions and deviations exist. Asian language verb systems are also regular. English, on the other hand, has many irregularities.

Speakers of AAL tend to regularize the verb structure . . .

Speakers of AAL tend to regularize the verb structure, primarily because the verb structure of their indigenous language is regularized. This results in many variations and differences in how the language is produced in relation to MAE. For example, the past tense of *be* in mainstream English results in *I was, you were, he was*. In accordance with its underlying Bantu structure, AAL regularizes this to *I was, you was, he was*. In mainstream English, *swim* is conjugated as *I swim, you swim, he swims*. But an African American speaker might say "Did you see Bobby swim? He *swim* good."

One of the most striking examples of the regularity rule is in the reflexive pronoun. The reflexive is produced in MAE by borrowing alternately from the possessive and the objective case. *Myself* comes from the possessive *my*. *Himself* comes from the objective *him*, and for *ourselves*, we go back to the possessive

AAL consistently employs the posssessive case for reflexive pronouns.

our. By contrast, AAL consistently employs the possessive case for reflexive pronouns. Instead of saying, "Johnny hurt *him*self," the speaker of AAL would say, "Johnny hurt *his*self." This tendency to regularize is consistent throughout the verb structure of AAL.

Perhaps the most misunderstood construct in AAL is the habitual *be*. Linguistic analysis has revealed that the deep structure of the use of this verb in AAL is not English but Niger-Congo.[11] In AAL, the verb *to be* is used to show temporal contexts or points in time. English has no such corollary.

These are some of the characteristic lingustic features of AAL which have been traced to Niger-Congo or Bantu language forms. When speakers of African American Language enter kindergarten, they manifest neither linguistic deviance nor linguistic deficiency. Rather, they arrive equipped with a language form whose deep structure is embodied in Niger-Congo or Bantu.

Just as we would not expect a child reared in a mainstream English environment to arrive at school speaking AAL, neither should we expect the reverse. We must avoid unfavorable interpretations of children who speak AAL. We must eschew saying they are not bright, or their parents did not teach them language, or that they can not learn when in fact they have learned language. Teachers must recognize that native speakers of AAL do not suffer from linguistic or cognitive deficiencies; rather they enjoy linguistic differences.

---

[8] See Alleyne (1971).

[9] See Alleyne (1971), Ladefoged (1964), Smith (1977),Welmers (1973).

[10] See Labov (1983).

[11] See Smith (1977).

Learning MAE while embracing AAL is one way to learn and understand the rules of MAE.

Chapter 5

Perspectives On Teaching Speakers Of African American Language (AAL)

One great American myth holds that African American Language can be corrected into Mainstream American English. "No Bobby, the word is *des-sa-ka,* not *des.*" Other than teaching the child a funny way to say *desk*, this approach does not work. The fact that African American students continue to score lower than all other ethnic groups on standardized tests of language and have the lowest scores on the verbal segments of the SAT attests to the inappropriateness of the traditional corrective approach. I believe this result occurs partly because African American children have not received structured intervention that teaches the rules of MAE and how they differ from the rules of AAL.

In the landmark King case from 1979, parents sued the Ann Arbor School District (Michigan) for neglecting to effectively educate their children by failing to consider their language was different from the language of instruction.[12] Dr. Geneva Smitherman, author of ***Talking and Testifying,*** detailed the history of AAL. The judge ruled that in light of the available research, it was unacceptable for Ann Arbor teachers not to have a clue about this language. Interviews with Ann Arbor's teachers revealed that educators lacked knowledge of any appropriate language strategies to use. So how could the district effectively educate these students?

> **Once we understand that the child has a rule-governed language system, then we realize that our objective is not to correct Mainstream English, but to facilitate the acquisition of this new language form. We move from language correction to second language acquisition; from language eradication to language addition.**

❈ Toni Morrison

The perspective that many African Americans speak a language whose structure is not English cries out for an overhaul of the traditional approach to teaching African American children by correcting them. The corrective model originates with the deficit perspective. Once we understand that the child has a rule-governed language system, then we realize that our objective is not to correct mainstream English, but to facilitate the acquisition of this new language form. We move from language correction to second language acquisition; from language eradication to language addition.

Some people feel AAL should not remain intact. Others, like myself, disagree. AAL is actually a beautiful language form: it gives voice to a people and their culture. Those of us who speak it, feel this way about it. Given that Toni Morrison's novels (for example, ***Song of Solomon, Beloved,*** and ***Jazz***) employ AAL, the language also wins Pulitzer and Nobel prizes.

By the way, MAE is also a beautiful language form. The issue is not language competition but language co-existence. Indeed, one language is not better than another. German is neither better nor worse than French. Nor is Scandinavian better or worse than Yoruba. Languages are the communication system of a people.

For those who feel AAL should be a dialect of English because it borrows the lexicon of English-should not mainstream English should be a dialect of French, since over four-fifths of the English vocabulary originates with that language?

The fact is, languages borrow, and they borrow lexicon in particular. For reasons rooted in the history of slavery in America, AAL borrows its

... we add MAE to the linguistic repertoire of speakers of AAL.

lexicon from English. But the systematic rules which govern the morphosyntax of AAL are closer to the rules that govern Bantu or Niger-Congo languages.

Thus, our goal is not to eradicate AAL. We must not devalue children who speak AAL. To the contrary, we should strive to help them become comfortable, competent learners who have a solid sense of self and recognize they can become bilingual or multilingual. That is, we add MAE to the linguistic repertoire of speakers of AAL.

[12] See Chambers (1983).

❈ The paradigm of the American classroom enforces a European base. Knowledge of MAE is necessary in order to score well on college entrance exams.

CHAPTER 6

FACILITATING A SHIFT IN LANGUAGE INSTRUCTION STRATEGIES

In a viable multi-cultural world, we should strive to embrace the cultures of all peoples. However, this lofty notion does not hold in most places in the world. In most societies, the group in power determines linguistic standards. If you were living in Kenya, your success and well-being would depend on your understanding of the culture and language of Kenya.

Likewise, the paradigms that dominate education in the United States center around a European base. Given this view of reality, if non-European students (Asians, Hispanics, African Americans) want to succeed in American society, they will probably need to acquire the language and culture of America's power base.

African American youngsters need to gain knowledge of the school culture and language form by which they will be judged by the "gatekeepers" of life's opportunities. If these students expect to attend college, they must demonstrate facility in mainstream English while in high school and on college entrance exams. We do children a disservice if we fail to acknowledge that Mainstream American English should be added to their linguistic repertoire.

Teachers should not attempt to eradicate a child's home language; to discuss eradication of language is to discuss eradication of culture and hence, the eradication of a people. When a teacher tells African American children they do not

know how to talk, this teacher conveys the sentiment that the parents of these children do not know how to talk either.

Years passed before [August Wilson] recognized that whenever he attempted to make his characters speak, the face of a teacher would appear to remind him that the language he submitted to paper was not writing.

Once I had the opportunity to attend a fireside chat with August Wilson, the award-winning playwright. When I asked him how he became such a prolific writer, he said for ten years he had suffered from writer's block. He had wanted to write plays but could not give voice to his characters. Years passed before August Wilson recognized that whenever he attempted to make his characters speak, the face of a teacher would appear to remind him that the language he submitted to paper was not writing. As a result, he felt that using his natural language was wrong and this affected him deeply. Finally, after a decade of being torn between mainstream English and his natural language, he decided to write from within. The dialogue of his characters began to flow naturally, and through the successful plays that followed—including ***Ma Rainey's Black Bottom, Two Trains Running, The Piano Lesson, Fences,*** and ***Seven Guitars***—August Wilson has helped to introduce Americans to the richness of African American Language.

...mainstream English as a second language is the only sensible approach to teach the language of instruction.

While linguists disagree on the origin of AAL, all agree that AAL is systematic and rule-governed. The rules are phonologically and morphosyntactically different from the rules that govern MAE. Therefore, mainstream English as a second language is the only sensible approach to teach the language of instruction.

❀ Listening Centers play and important role in classroom instruction. They provide opportunities for students to hear mainstream English modeled daily

CHAPTER 7

GOALS AND STRATEGIES FOR MAINSTREAM ENGLISH MASTERY

Teaching speakers of African American Language to master Mainstream American English requires a strategy that bridges both languages. To this end, we have developed a strategy spanning grades K through 8—*English for Your Success*. Each student in this program seeks to achieve twelve sequential language development goals:

Ꮗ Develop an appreciation of/for the language and culture of the home.

Ꮗ Develop receptive language in MAE.

Ꮗ Acquire basic literacy skills.

Ꮗ Develop an awareness and appreciation of diversity.

Ꮗ Recognize and label the differences between AAL and MAE.

Ꮗ Expand students' personal thesaurus of conceptually coded word concepts.

Ꮗ Analyze the linguistic differences between AAL and MAE.

Ꮗ Use MAE structure functionally in oral and written form.

Ꮗ Recognize the language requirements of different situations.

Ꮗ Demonstrate the proficient use ofMAE in oral and written form.

Ꮗ Demonstrate an expanded knowledge and appreciation of the language and culture of the home and of others.

Ꮗ Communicate effectively in cross-cultural environments.

Each of these goals is described on the following pages, along with basic strategies for implementing the goals.

GOAL 1—Develop an Appreciation of (for) the Language and Culture of the Home

The language and culture of children form a foundation for academic achievement. Because most African American children spend their early years in families whose culture and language are uniquely African American, it is critical that these students develop an appreciation of their culture. One approach is to infuse the student's history and culture into the curriculum. The teacher who makes effective use of this approach has access to a rich variety of cultural materials and literature that reflect African American culture and language. Daily, the teacher infuses culturally meaningful activities into the curriculum. In addition, the classroom and school maintain cultural centers that feature art and artifacts, games, costumes and clothing, posters, pictorial histories, etc. By learning of the extraordinary contributions Africans and African Americans have made to world history and culture, students develop a positive outlook toward themselves.

A second approach used to implement this goal is to incorporate the home, parent, and community in a supportive relationship with the educational process. The validation of African American Language requires the validation of the home and community in which the language is rooted. Actions that promote parent and community involvement include taking students on field trips within the community and having the school sponsor community activities such as career days, parent *exposés*, cultural festivals, and after-school programs. Schools encourage parents to volunteer at school, and teachers make effective use of local resources such as newspapers, local field trip sites, and community members. When schools embrace parents as partners in the educational process, students' attitudes and academic development climb.

This goal may also be supported by engaging literature that offers students a glimpse into themselves and their culture and makes connections between them, their homes, their communities, and the world at large. Schools are encouraged to use literature that reflects the students' home life, personal interest, cultural background and language. Students read culturally appropriate materials every day. Teachers use class sets of core books. Classroom libraries contain a wide variety of literature including magazines, newspapers, books and student work. African Americans are featured prominently in both historical and contemporary settings. Print materials span a range of reading levels and a variety of interests. This literature motivates and encourages students to become active participants in a learning experience to which they can easily relate.

Home

GOAL 2—Develop Receptive Language in MAE

Because language is acquired subconsciously, effortlessly, and intuitively, teachers of African American students must expose these students to MAE throughout the instructional day. Through continual exposure, students begin to intuit the rules and discourse patterns of the language. The teacher, as she delivers instruction, represents the most consistent verbal model of MAE language production for the student. Yet, she need not be the only model. By incorporating multiple media into the delivery of information and engaging students kinesthetically, visually, and through hearing, the teacher ensures that students make meaningful connections to the curriculum. Students grasp the lessons immediately because the subject matter is relevant and the instructional materials are compelling. Also, cooperative learning strategies can be used to engage students in a variety of language-rich learning activities that encourage students to practice MAE while enhancing their understanding of the subject matter.

Receptive Language

English for Your Success emphasizes six approaches for developing receptive language in MAE. One approach is for teachers to use multiple modality teaching techniques in the classroom. Instruction is continually infused with multimedia resources, instructional television, and visual stimuli. The teacher allows students to physically participate in activities, including lots of hands-on science and math activities and investigations. The teacher uses a variety of modes (e.g. auditory, visual, kinesthetic, tactile) to present each lesson and activity. The teacher facilitates student production of multimedia reports and visual displays, for example.

Second, the teacher provides opportunities for instructional conversations in MAE to encourage student-to-student and teacher-to-student interactions in a collaborative learning context and to provide models of the target language. The teacher sets up cooperative groups, peer tutoring and editing, and small group projects and activities. Students write daily. Non-mainstream and mainstream English speakers are grouped together to facilitate cooperation and dialogue.

Receptive Language

A third approach is to engage students in authentic learning activities incorporating materials matched to their interests and ability level. Hands-on activities in the various content areas utilizing concrete materials and manipulatives are used throughout the school day.

A fourth approach for pursuing this goal is to emphasize vocabulary development with a focus on synonyms. Vocabulary development is viewed as a natural process that occurs when students use language to communicate ideas. The teacher encourages vocabulary development in the context of communicating ideas.

Students keep personal dictionaries to record new words. The teacher praises and values students' use of new vocabulary.

The fifth approach uses literature to provide opportunities for consistent exposure to the target language. Students are read to every day and are given frequent opportunities to explore multiple discourse patterns and styles in MAE such as narrative, poetry, fairy tales, science fiction, and non-fiction. The teacher uses appropriate voices when reading different characters. The use of instructional media makes literature more accessible to students who are not proficient in MAE. Finally, students are given ample opportunity to speak and write in a variety of discourse patterns.

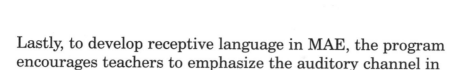

Lastly, to develop receptive language in MAE, the program encourages teachers to emphasize the auditory channel in learning activities. Students are allowed to hear effective models of the target language (MAE). The teacher encourages oral mastery of MAE and accepts all written and spoken responses in AAL. The teacher does not overtly correct AAL at the moment it is spoken except through repetitive modeling. For example, if a student says, "I ain't got no paper," the teacher might respond, "No, you don't have any paper. Let me get some for you."

Receptive Language

GOAL 3—Acquire Basic Literacy Skills

Because the homes of many African American students are dominated by oral language communication, the school must play a key role in helping students acquire basic literacy skills through balancing oral and written instruction and materials.

EYS offers six approaches for developing basic literacy skills in students. First, the program incorporates "whole language" approaches using information and materials from the students' culture to establish realistic contexts for language experiences. Language mastery is viewed as a constructive process involving reading and writing authentic, communicative-based materials. Students learn to read by reading and they learn to write by writing. The teacher uses literature extensively. Students do their skill lessons in context. Language projects, which may extend days or weeks, result in books, stories, and plays published by students.

A second approach is to create a "print-rich" classroom environment that includes teacher-and student-generated lists, newspapers, maps, charts, magazines, resources, books, and a classroom library that reflects students' home language and culture. A wide variety of printed materials are displayed throughout the classroom and students have easy access to them. Books feature African American children and families. Books, newspapers, and magazines reflect students' personal lives and interests. Materials span a variety of grade levels. The teacher and the school value work produced by students.

A third approach involves using small group activities (cooperative and mediated learning) to encourage language development and the sharing of ideas and learning strategies. Students are encouraged to communicate during group projects and activities. To ensure equal participation, students rotate through various roles as editors, typists, readers, and speakers.

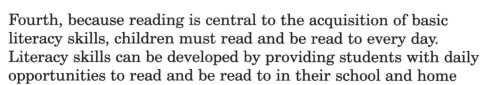

Fourth, because reading is central to the acquisition of basic literacy skills, children must read and be read to every day. Literacy skills can be developed by providing students with daily opportunities to read and be read to in their school and home environment. Sustained silent reading should occur for at least 20 minutes a day, plus daily time for the teacher to read aloud to students. Reading corners, story nooks, and author's chairs make reading more enjoyable. Students read aloud to other students and the teacher. A school-wide reading program provides tutoring within classrooms and across grade levels. At home, parents should reinforce school work by reading to their children and listening as their children read to them. Through parent classes and workshops, parents can be encouraged to support positive classroom experiences at home.

Fifth, the program encourages the teacher to use technology as a tool in language and literacy acquisition. Children who use computer word processors write more and write better. Students use classroom computers (at least one computer for every five students) for word processing and language development activities. Students use electronic spellers and thesauruses to look up words. Classroom listening centers feature literature titles on tape. The teacher also makes frequent use of television in conjunction with video and laser disk players.

Sixth, literacy acquisition occurs more rapidly if the teacher integrates oral and written language into all curricular areas. Students write daily in their journals. They write in math, science, history, art, and even sports. The teacher provides students with frequent opportunities to share their writing and to make oral presentations to the class.

GOAL 4—Develop an Awareness and Appreciation of Diversity

We live in a world in which technology advances rapidly and business is becoming increasingly global. In the world of the 21st Century, American students—including African American students—will be required to communicate effectively in a variety of settings and cross-cultural contexts. The cultivation of cultural fluency in students begins with the development of understanding and appreciation of diversity. By gaining an awareness and appreciation of their own cultural uniqueness, African American students can explore and develop respect for the similarities and differences among cultures.

The teacher can use several approaches to implement this goal. For example, the teacher could take advantage of the various languages and cultures represented in the school and classroom to help students understand and appreciate diversity. The teacher should recognize and acknowledge all children in the classroom and allow for open discussions of the different languages and cultures represented. The teacher can also facilitate cooperative and collaborative study of cultures involving students, parents, family members, faculty, staff, and other classroom visitors.

Second, the teacher can use multicultural artifacts, literature, arts, crafts, music, and holidays to foster students' awareness and appreciation of diversity. Students inspect and analyze actual artifacts, arts, and crafts within the classroom. Music and literature from around the world is used and valued. Students explore content area subjects like math, history, and science by studying the achievements and contributions of different cultures throughout history.

Third, the teacher can provide opportunities for students to explore their own cultural uniqueness and to identify and respect the similarities and differences among other cultures.

Under the guidance of the teacher, students compare and contrast the different cultures and languages represented in the classroom. Students develop an understanding of the unique experiences of African Americans. Students use multicultural resources to gain insights into the subtleties of other cultures. Students examine ways in which African American culture resembles or differs from "mainstream" culture as well as cultures from around the world.

Diversity

In a fourth approach, the teacher introduces students to the practical dynamics of interacting effectively with diverse cultural groups. Students explore the language requirements of various situations and investigate the language needs of different social contexts through role-playing and dramatic play. Students discuss the implications of language use in different contexts, such as in school, in a doctor's office, at the playground, or at a police station.

GOAL 5—Recognize and Label the Differences Between AAL and MAE

Through understanding the differences and similarities between AAL and MAE, students develop proficiency in MAE and thereby develop into bilingual, bicultural members of society. One approach the teacher uses to implement this goal is to provide opportunities for students to compare and contrast the linguistic features of MAE and AAL. Because the teacher does not elevate one language over the other, students view both languages as valid.

Differences

Secondly, because students learn best in a meaningful, authentic, relevant context, the teacher takes advantage of "teachable moments" throughout the school day to explore the differences between AAL and MAE. That is, language learning occurs not only during the designated language arts period, but takes place throughout the instructional day. The teacher might use students' content-specific oral or written language productions to highlight AAL-MAE differences while reinforcing the concepts being taught in the content area subject. In addition, language breaks are taken periodically throughout the instructional day.

Thirdly, because African American students tend to write what they say, rough drafts of their written work often feature elements of the home language. Therefore, the editing phase of the writing process provides another critical teachable moment that the teacher could use to reinforce student awareness of the linguistic differences between the two languages.

GOAL 6—Expand Students' Personal Thesaurus of Conceptually-Coded Word Concepts

AAL often uses a single word or phrase to convey varied meanings or concepts depending on where (the context) and how (inflection or emphasis) the word is spoken. On the other hand, MAE possesses many different words that convey the same or a similar meaning.

Personal Thesaurus

For instance, an African American child might use the word *bad* to convey different meanings. "Johnny was bein' *bad*" could mean that Johnny was misbehaving. "Johnny feel *bad*" could mean that he is ill or that he is apologetic. "That car look *bad*" could mean the car looks good, attractive, or beautiful; or it could mean that the car looks very unattractive. "You betta not mess with him. Dude is *bad*. . ." could mean that the boy fights proficiently. A mainstream English expression for each of these uses of the word *bad* might draw upon a variety of words for use with any one of the concepts.

The teacher should view this aspect of AAL as a strength when carrying out EYS approaches for implementing this goal. For one, the teacher provides students with multiple opportunities for exposure to MAE discourse style. Students recite speeches, debate issues, participate in short plays and read scripts that feature MAE. The teacher encourages students to play roles that generally require MAE, such as newscasters, reporters, advertisements, and television commercials.

Second, the teacher focuses on vocabulary development with an emphasis on synonyms, antonyms, prefixes, and suffixes. Vocabulary development centers on students' own experiences, whether culled from the literature or from the students' lives. Words are examined in context and the dictionary is used only to verify or support student-generated word meanings. The expectation is that students will integrate new words and concepts into their vocabularies by connecting them to their store of personal experiences in AAL and culture.

GOAL 7—Analyze the Linguistic Differences Between AAL and MAE

Having developed the ability to recognize the differences between the home language and MAE, African American students can begin to compare and contrast the linguistic structures of AAL and MAE. Students develop a keener sense of both MAE and AAL without elevating the status of one language above the other. The teacher reinforces the equal status of the languages by helping students understand that AAL and MAE represent two distinct languages, each governed by its own set of rules.

Linguistic Differences

Here the teacher uses a variety of literary works to compare and contrast the linguistic features of AAL and MAE. Students explore six to ten literature titles throughout the school year. These titles feature African and African American people, culture, and language.

A second approach involves the use of samples of students' daily oral and written language to compare and contrast AAL and MAE. The teacher validates students' oral and written language in a positive, affirming classroom environment in which all language is valued. Students' oral and written language is used in structured contrasting analysis lessons. AAL is translated to MAE and MAE is translated to AAL.

GOAL 8—Use MAE Structure Functionally in Oral and Written Form

As African American students gain proficiency with the structure of MAE language, the teacher guides students through numerous opportunities to practice MAE functionally in a variety of real or imagined contexts. This way, students develop self-confidence in using MAE as they begin to develop an awareness of situations where MAE is required for effective communication.

MAE

EYS offers three approaches for implementing this goal. One, the teacher uses oral language activities to promote the development of MAE. Students recite speeches, participate in debates, hold moot court and mock trials, participate in plays and theater productions that feature MAE, and role-play situations that require MAE (newscasters, reporters, advertisements and commercials). The teacher places emphasis on whole language strategies.

Two, the teacher employs written language activities to promote the development of MAE. Students write daily. Students maintain several writing journals for a variety of subjects. Writing portfolios are utilized to chronicle the development of writing and MAE proficiency.

Three, the teacher provides students with opportunities to compare and practice MAE oral and written discourse patterns. Students recite speeches, debate issues, participate in short plays and read scripts that feature MAE. Written discourse patterns are observed through extensive use of literary works. Graphic organizers are employed to facilitate MAE written discourse patterns.

GOAL 9—Recognize the Language Requirements of Different Situations

Students continue to expand their awareness of the sometimes subtle situations when they must use MAE to communicate effectively. Increased exposure to MAE models sharpens students' analysis of the language requirements in a variety of situations. Students begin to focus on the oral discourse patterns of AAL and MAE, strengthening their fluency in MAE and providing validation for the home language.

Situational

EYS employs three approaches to achieve this goal. One, the teacher provides a variety of situations for students to judge and select language for effective communication. Students take on various roles in realistic situations requiring both AAL and MAE. Students develop and share skits and video presentations and take field trips to observe authentic situations where judgments must be made about when to use AAL and when to use MAE. Two, the teacher introduces students to the oral communication patterns of AAL and MAE and provides opportunities for their use. The two languages are valued equally, so classroom time for using both is provided through literature featuring one or both languages, content area exploration, brainstorming sessions, full class discussions, role playing, and dramatic activities, for example. Three, the teacher provides opportunities for students to observe MAE models outside the classroom, placing greater emphasis on authentic experiences related to the curriculum, such as multiple school journeys, like walking field trips. These experiences coupled with exposure to outside experts and opportunities, such as career days and interactions should be with local business representatives, community leaders, and board members.

GOAL 10—Demonstrate the Proficient Use of MAE In Oral and Written Form

Mastery of MAE requires real experiences in which students are able to show they know when and how to speak and write MAE. These experiences help to develop the self-confidence and self-assurance students need in order to accelerate the process by which they increase their fluency in MAE.

Demonstrate the Proficient Uses

To implement this goal, the teacher provides students with opportunities to demonstrate continued mastery in MAE using a variety of writing domains. Students engage in daily, weekly, and monthly writing activities. Students are encouraged to write for specific audiences, each requiring the use of MAE to get their message across. Students write advertising copy to sell products, op-ed pieces to argue and debate a viewpoint, speeches, dramatic scripts, and news stories for both print and electronic media.

Also, the teacher offers students multiple opportunities—formal and informal—to demonstrate oral mastery of MAE. Students work in cooperative groups to discuss issues and key concepts throughout the instructional day. Students role-play different situations that involve use of MAE. Students take advantage of home study activities and volunteer work that provide authentic experiences for MAE use.

GOAL 11—Demonstrate an Expanded Knowledge and Appreciation of the Language and Culture of the Home and of Others

Because many African American families live in racially isolated communities, few opportunities exist for the children in these families to interact with other cultural groups. Schools are one environment where African American children can acquire knowledge and understanding of others who look or talk differently than they do. An anti-bias curriculum, guided field trips throughout their own and other communities, instructional videos and television, and cultural festivals are other examples of activities designed to heighten multicultural awareness.

Language and Culture of the Home and of Others

The three approaches employed by *EYS* to implement this goal take students through knowing, appreciating, and respecting cultural differences. First, students examine the similarities and differences within their primary culture. By examining culture from both a contemporary and historical perspective, students make connections more easily. Students analyze demographic and geographic differences throughout African American culture.

Second, students examine the similarities and differences between cultures. As much as possible, students compare and contrast cultures in the context of the established curriculum, rather than as a separate subject. Through this method, the study of cultural differences (such as in games, clothing, dance, and rituals) takes place in science, math, history, art, and music, as well as language arts.

Students' knowledge of and within various cultures helps to create a school and classroom environment that respects multiculturalism. The concepts of multiculturalism, anti-bias, and respect for diversity are infused in the curriculum through comparative and cooperative analyses of the contributions various cultures have made to history, art, science, education, literature, mathematics, and other areas. The school sponsors days for the various cultures represented in the student population. Individuals from various cultural backgrounds interact with students inside and outside the classroom and the school.

Language and Culture of the Home and of Others

GOAL 12—Communicate Effectively in Cross-Cultural Environments

Once African American students have acquired literacy, moved toward mastery of MAE, and developed an appreciation for their own language and culture as well as that of other diverse languages and cultures, they will operate as bilingual, culturally fluent individuals able to access post-secondary education and career opportunities in a global economy. Students' experiences as educated, productive members of society will provide them with continued reinforcement and increased proficiency in mainstream English throughout their adult lives.

Communicate

To implement this goal, students use real-life situations to examine communicative effectiveness in different cultural contexts. Students become increasingly fluent in multiple cultures and seek out multiple opportunities to communicate in a variety of situations and cultural contexts including school-to-work programs, volunteer work, writing articles for local newspapers, and communicating with political representatives and business leaders, (e.g. making presentations to the local board of education). Students share their experiences with the class and with their families.

⚮ By actively practicing the twelve goals, students will be in a better frame of mind to pursue MAE mastery

CHAPTER 8
SAMPLE STUDENT LESSONS AND LESSON ORGANIZER

By recognizing and appreciating their home language, students will be in a much better cognitive position and frame of mind to pursue mastery of Mainstream American English—be it written or oral, formal or informal. By systematically and relentlessly pursuing the twelve goals using the recommended approaches, schools and educators can help speakers of African American Language master MAE. Moreover, by achieving these goals, students enrich their understanding of both AAL and MAE.

Sample Student Lessons

A variety of sample lesson plans are provided in grade-level teacher handbooks that teachers can use in conjunction with this handbook. Table 1 summarizes the coverage of these grade-level handbooks. One handbook will provide lesson plans for grades K-1 for the first four goals of *English for Your Success.* A second teacher handbook provides lesson plans for grades 2-3 that focus on goals one through eight. The third and fourth teacher handbooks provide lesson plans for grades 4-5 and 6-8, respectively, that cover all 12 goals of *EYS.*

This section provides examples of lessons that teachers have used to carry out these goals and thereby aid African-American students in developing fluency in MAE. Each lesson focuses on one or more of the 12 goals and uses multiple approaches or strategies for carrying out the goal(s). We include one lesson for grades K-1, one for grades 2-3, one for grades 4-5 and one for grades 6-8.

Following the sample student lessons is a *Lesson Organizer* for teachers' use. This form was designed for teachers to copy and use to write their own lessons. The form is organized into the same basic structure as the sample lessons and follows the process and sequence used in the Los Angeles program.

Table 1: English for Your Success

Goals	Grade Level			
	K-1	2-3	4-5	6-8
1. Acquire an awareness and appreciation of home language and culture	▼	▼	▼	▼
2. Develop receptive language in MAE	▼	▼	▼	▼
3. Acquire basic literacy skills	▼	▼	▼	▼
4. Develop an awareness and appreciation of language and cultural diversity	▼	▼	▼	▼
5. Be able to recognize and label the differences between AAL and MAE		▼	▼	▼
6. Expand a personal thesaurus of conceptually coded word concepts		▼	▼	▼
7. Analyze linguistic differences between MAE and AAL		▼	▼	▼
8. Use MAE structure functionally in oral and written form		▼	▼	▼
9. Recognize the language requirements of different situations		▼	▼	▼
10. Demonstrate proficient use of MAE in written and oral form			▼	▼
11. Develop an expanded knowledge and appreciation of AAL and the language and culture of others			▼	▼
12. Communicate effectively in cross-cultural environments			▼	▼

GOALS

Using the book *Tell Me a Story, Mama*, pupils will:

demonstrate that they are acquiring basic literacy skills;

use synonyms to help describe relationships and mathematics and science concepts;

develop their personal vocabularies;

enjoy exposure to Mainstream American English (MAE);

enjoy and appreciate literature.

Materials to Prepare

for each child in the group,

- **photos** of their family members, especially grandmothers and grandfathers, or magazines with representative photos
- **paper**
- **crayons**
- **safety scissors**
- **non-toxic glue**

to use with the group,

- a copy of the book *Tell Me a Story, Mama*
- **chalkboard** or **classroom** chart to write on
- **bulletin board decorated with multicultural families** including a variety of family situations reflecting the pupils in your class. Be sure to include extended family situations with grandparents and others. These may be photographs or illustrations
- **at least one of the following books** in a reading or story center or table so that pupils could continue the activity with other books:

    The Dancing Granny, retold and illustrated by Ashley Bryan,

    Big Mama, The Patchwork Quilt by Valerie Flournoy

    If You Give a Mouse a Cokie, The Doorbell Rang

Materials to Prepare for Cross Curricular Links

(V) Visitor's Day prepare a letter and make necessary school arrangements to have a Grandparent's Day in your classroom

(LA) LanguageArts paper, crayons, photos or illustrations to use in a family tree book that pupils create stapler or brads to fasten the books together

(M) Math a recipe for cookies, measuring utensils, and all the ingredients. You will also need a way to bake the cookies so that pupils may enjoy them. chart paper for graphing

(M) (A) Math and Art paper, crayons, large butcher paper (enough to glue or tape into a sheet that will hold one picture by each child) glue

PREREADING Discuss families with pupils, asking questions such as

What is a grandmother?

What do grandmothers do in a family?

Are there grandmothers on the bulletin board?

Where are they?

How do you know?

Tell pupils you are going to read a story about families. Show pupils a picture of the grandmother in the book.
Ask pupils to predict what the grandmother will do in the book.

chart or chalkboard

On the chalkboard or a clean page of a classroom chart, write down pupils' predictions. Tell pupils that you will read the book and then look back at their predictions to see how close they were.

Encourage vocabulary development by discussing words that pupils call their grandmothers and words that make pupils think of grandmothers. Write these down for review after reading the book, also.

46

GUIDED READING AND ACTIVITIES

As you read the book aloud, show the pictures and discuss pupils' reactions to the grandmother. Encourage pupils to predict what will happen in upcoming pages in the book as you progress. Discuss the family role grandmothers play.

Review pupils' predictions that you wrote down. Discuss the ways in which pupils were correct, and discuss what happened in the book to ensure that all pupils understood the book.

Review the words pupils generated about grandmothers.

Ask pupils

Did you learn other words in the story about grandmothers?

What were these words?

Were there names for grandmother?

What do you call a grandmother?

What are words that tell about a grandmother?

Add these words to the class or group list.

Have pupils make a family tree picture of themselves and various extended family members. You may wish to have pupils use actual photos which they have brought and their parents have agreed to let the children cut/glue, etc., or you may wish to use these photos on the classroom bulletin board, and have pupils continue this activity by drawing themselves and family members. Write or help pupils write at least one synonym and one descriptive word on their family tree to demonstrate a new word added to their vocabulary. If time permits, have pupils present their pictures to their classmates and explain why they chose the word on their picture.

Continue the activity by setting up and using a reading table or area for other family-related members with one or more of the books listed in **Materials to Prepare**. As time permits, continue the grandmother activity with the additional books, discussing synonyms and descriptive words.

VISITOR'S DAY

(V) Invite grandparents to the classroom for part of a special Grandparent's Day. Share cookies with the grandparents. Invite one or more grandparent to read a story to the class. Encourage students to interview their grandparents about similarities and differences in being a child in the past and today.

CROSS CURRICULAR LINKS

LANGUAGE ARTS

(LA) Have pupils make additional family tree pictures, or incorporate their pictures into a family tree book. Help pupils write synonyms and descriptive words about families.

MATHEMATICS

(M) Make cookies that pupils name "Granny Cookies," "Poppy Cookies," or another family name to share with each other and with their families. To start, ask pupils to name their favorite type of cookie. Graph the responses so that pupils can tell which is the most liked, least liked, and so on on the graphing paper. Discuss how the graph shows the favorite class cookie. Then, help pupils make one type of cookie, showing them how to measure each ingredient. The teacher should measure ingredients that are difficult for pupils to handle. Discuss measurement terms as each measurement occurs, showing pupils what each unit is. Discuss which units are larger and which are smaller units. Discuss the mathematical concepts of more and less by asking pupils whether more or less of an ingredient is needed to reach the line or fill point on the measuring utensil.

SCIENCE

(S) Discuss the concepts of solid and liquid, and the fact that substances can change form, while making the "Granny Cookies."

MATHEMATICS AND ART

(M) (A) Pupils may draw illustrations of their grandmothers or other family members on paper and then glue their pictures onto a large sheet of butcher paper to form a family quilt. Before pupils glue their pictures, discuss what the pattern will be, helping pupils design a recurring pattern that will be symmetrical and pleasing to the eye.

THE TALKING EGGS
by Robert D. San Souci, illustrated by Jerry Pickney

GOALS

Using the book *The Talking Eggs*, pupils will:

discuss animals that are oviparous *(from eggs)*
and the differences in their eggs;

be able to recognize and label the differences between
African American Language and Mainstream American English by:

- comparing and contrasting the oral and written components of AAL and MAE;

- using teachable moments during content instruction to identify and explain language differences;

- using the editing step in the writing process to address differences between AAL and MAE.

Materials to Prepare

for each child in the group,

- **plastic hosiery egg** with 3 or more items in each, such as **pennies, beans, beads, paper**, etc.

- **paper** and **crayons**

to use with the group,

- copy of the book ***The Talking Eggs***
- **a chalkboard** or **large easel** with paper on which you can make a chart with two columns, listing the children's names down one column and the contents of each child's egg in the other column.
- sentence strips with phrases in AAL on them from ***The Talking Eggs***.
- sentence strips with the AAL phrases translated into MAE.
- **a pocket chart** to hold the sentence strips, or tape to display. them on the board as you discuss them

Materials to Prepare **for Cross Curricular Links**

S **Science** a copy of the book *Chickens Aren't the Only Ones*, and/or pictures of the life cycles of various animals that come from eggs

S **Science** photos or pictures of farms, farm animals, and wild animals

G **Geography** a map of the United States

PREREADING Discuss eggs with pupils, asking questions encouraging curiosity, such as

What is inside an egg?

What did you expect to find inside an egg?

✂ Give each pupil a plastic hosiery egg with different contents.

As pupils open their eggs, write down the contents of each pupil's egg on the chart or chalkboard, and discuss them with the group:

Were you surprised?

Can different eggs have different things inside?

When?

Why?

Tell students that you are going to read a folktale from Louisiana about some eggs and what is in them. Show pupils the cover of the book *The Talking Eggs* and ask them to predict what the book will be about.
On the chalkboard or a clean page of the chart, write down pupils' predictions.
Tell pupils that you will read the book and then look back at their predictions to see how close they were.

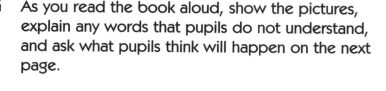

GUIDED READING

As you read the book aloud, show the pictures, explain any words that pupils do not understand, and ask what pupils think will happen on the next page.

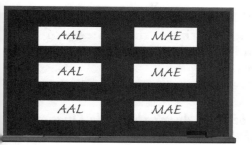

Put the sentence strips of AAL on the left side of the pocket chart or board and the MAE strips on the right, mixing the MAE strips so that they do not give pupils the translation of the AAL strip beside them. As you talk about each AAL strip with pupils, ensure that they remember which character said the sentence or phrase and that they understood the context in the story. Have students match the AAL strips with their correct MAE translations. Discuss the skill of the author in using AAL and MAE to tell a story and make it interesting. (Extension: If pupils progress rapidly, you may wish to hold back one or two AAL sentence strips and have pupils do their own translations, writing those on blank sentence strips.)

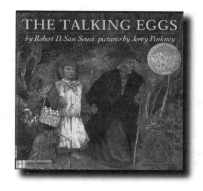

Continue the activity by having pupils compare and contrast the outside appearances and contents of the eggs in the story. Help pupils write their own sentences to describe the eggs, then have pupils draw corresponding pictures. Encourage pupils to identify whether their sentences are AAL or MAE.

CROSS CURRICULAR LINKS

LANGUAGE ARTS

(LA) Have pupils role-play their favorite parts of *The Talking Eggs*. Encourage the use of both AAL and MAE. Help pupils create story and word webs based on *The Talking Eggs*.

MATHEMATICS

(M) Have pupils sort, classify, and count the contents of the plastic eggs.

Have pupils arrange the contents of the plastic eggs in order of size, from smallest to largest.

Help pupils measure the size of the contents of the plastic eggs and write the numbers on a chart from smallest to largest.

SCIENCE

(S) Using the book *Chickens Aren't the Only Ones*, and/or pictures of the life cycles of various animals that come from eggs, compare and contrast animals that are oviparous. Help pupils make a chart listing their comparisons and contrasts.

Show pupils pictures of farm and wild animals.

Discuss which animals pupils think come from eggs.

GEOGRAPHY

(G) Using the map of the United States, help pupils identify the setting of the story (Louisiana) and use the map scale to help you figure out how far away Louisiana is from their state. If you are in Louisiana, help pupils figure out how far Louisiana is from locations where they have relatives or have visited or heard of.

ART

(A) Pupils may decorate the plastic eggs with art materials.

GOALS

By role-playing and interviewing famous
African Americans, students will:

demonstrate functional use of MAE orally and in writing;

recognize and label the differences between AAL and MAE;

practice literacy skills;

develop receptive language in MAE;

communicate effectively in cross-cultural environments; and

develop an understanding and appreciation of AAL
and culture.

Materials to Prepare

for each student in the group,

  paper

pencil

to use with the group,

- television, video equipment for playing a movie, and the
  movie, ***The Autobiography of Miss Jane Pittman***

- Classroom chart or chalkboard
  (note: this activity will take time and should be
  scheduled carefully)

Materials to Prepare **for Cross Curricular Links**

- **Language Arts** research or access to appropriate
  reference materials

- **Audio/Video** tape recorder blank tapes or videotaping equipment
  if available

DISCUSSION

Explain to students that interviewing is a fun and useful skill that requires good oral language and listening skills. Tell pupils that they should prepare to become interviewers in class by observing what good interviewers do. Discuss some interviewing techniques and questions with which students have experience. If time permits, assign observation of interviews with professional interviewers to students as an overnight or classroom activity, e.g. Black Entertainment Television (BET), magazine interviews, and radio interviews.

Explain that the class will now watch the movie *The Autobiography of Miss Jane Pittman*. After watching the movie, the class will role-play an interview with Miss Jane Pittman. Suggest that as students watch the movie, they think of and note question topics to explore with Miss Jane Pittman.

Show the movie to the class.

Discuss the movie and the students' reactions to Miss Jane and her experiences. You may need to help students understand differences between today and the time of Miss Jane Pittman's experiences. Encourage students to make lists of AAL and MAE and translate each one to the other.

chart or chalkboard

Have students generate their interview questions and list them on the chalkboard or class chart. Refer to students' observations of professional interviews with professional interviewers. Discuss good interview techniques to keep in mind, such as listening carefully, body language, and researching the subject before conducting the interview.

Have pairs of students take turns interviewing and role-playing Miss Jane Pittman. Give a time limit to each interview, and encourage group suggestions for improving interviews. Encourage a supportive atmosphere in which constructive criticism and encouragement are offered for all students. Encourage students to use MAE and AAL appropriately and effectively. Allow students to rely on their written notes.

CROSS CURRICULAR LINKS

LANGUAGE ARTS

LA Encourage students to read the biography of a famous African American and have them discuss it with the class. If time permits, have students write and role-play interviews with the subject of the biography they read. Good candidates are Thurgood Marshall and Harriet Tubman.

Students may also interview a local community leader or leader in education in their school. Encourage thorough preparation for the interviews and, if possible, videotape or audiotape them for playback and sharing with others.

TECHNOLOGY

T Students may create their own African American biography and design or format it on the computer for class presentation or inclusion in their portfolios.

MATHEMATICS, SCIENCE, AND OTHER CURRICULUM AREAS

M Integrate this lesson with other curriculum areas such as mathematics, science, engineering, medicine, literature, and the visual and performing arts by having students, either individually or in pairs or groups, research a famous African American in the field and prepare an interview with her or him. If available, use videotape equipment to videotape the student interviews.

GOALS

In this lesson students will:

use Mainstream American English (MAE) functionally in oral and written forms by **role playing** newscasters, announcers, or other media roles;

engage in total modality learning by using audio-visual aids such as tape recorders and video recorders;

engage in authentic learning activities, selecting materials matching their interests;

emphasize auditory learning styles in oral MAE activities;

use real-life situations to judge and select the appropriate language for effecive communication, MAE or AAL.

Materials to Prepare
to use with the group,

- **Two video or audio tapes** prepared beforehand, one of people speaking in authentic AAL and one of a newscast with people (including African Americans) speaking MAE

- **Appropriate equipment** to play the two tapes for the class

- **A current newspaper**

Optional

- **Video** or **audio** taping equipment for students to use

Materials to Prepare **for Cross Curricular Links**

- **Social Studies** research materials and library tim

- **Art** materials to create a mural

- **Math** calculators and graph paper; if available, spreadsheet software to create graphs and tables

Organize students into cooperative learning groups.

Play the two tapes for all the groups.

Lead a discussion about the language in each.

Contrast the language and use of AAL and MAE. Explore the different uses of language in different situations.

Discuss why students might use different languages in different situations.

Introduce the concept of code-switching, or switching to appropriate language for effective communication depending on the situation.

Have each cooperative group analyze the use of MAE in the tape of a newscast and in newspapers. Have each group make their own analytical list of how, why, and when MAE is used effectively to communicate. Allow time for each group to present their list to the class and to discuss group responses.

Next, have each group prepare their own newscast that uses both MAE and AAL appropriately. Have each group give their media presentation and discuss with the class how it uses language. Encourage role-play. If you have video or audio taping equipment available, tape the group presentations for playback.

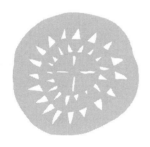

CROSS CURRICULAR LINKS

Harriet Tubman

Frederick Douglass

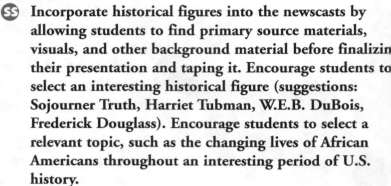
W.E.B.DuBois

SOCIAL STUDIES

 Incorporate historical figures into the newscasts by allowing students to find primary source materials, visuals, and other background material before finalizin their presentation and taping it. Encourage students to select an interesting historical figure (suggestions: Sojourner Truth, Harriet Tubman, W.E.B. DuBois, Frederick Douglass). Encourage students to select a relevant topic, such as the changing lives of African Americans throughout an interesting period of U.S. history.

ART

A Students may design a mural about their newscasts or about the historical figures included in their tapes.

MATHEMATICS

M Encourage students to prepare and include statistical tables and graphs in their newscasts.

ENGLISH FOR YOUR SUCCESS LESSON ORGANIZER

LESSON TITLE _____

GRADE LEVEL _____

GOALS
(check one)

1. ☐ Acquire an awareness and appreciation of home language and culture

2. ☐ Develop receptive language in Mainstream American English

3. ☐ Acquire basic literacy skills

4. ☐ Develop an awareness and appreciation of language and cultural diversity

5. ☐ Be able to recognize and label the differences between African American Language and Mainstream American English

6. ☐ Expand a personal thesaurus of conceptually coded word concepts

7. ☐ Analyze linguistic differences between Mainstream American English and African American Language

8. ☐ Use Mainstream American English structure functionally in oral and written form

9. ☐ Recognize the language requirements of different situations

10. ☐ Demonstrate proficient use of Mainstream American English in written and oral form

11. ☐ Develop an expanded knowledge and appreciation of African American language and the language and culture of others

12. ☐ Communicate effectively in cross-cultural environments

STRATEGIES AND APPROACHES
List the strategies and approaches by which the goal will be achieved.

STUDENT PRODUCT/CULMINATING TASK
What will students produce to demonstrate proficiency or achievement?

Materials to Prepare

■ **for each child in the group**

■ **to use with the group or class**

Materials to Prepare for Cross Curricular Links

Curriculum Area	Materials

ENGLISH FOR YOUR SUCCESS *LESSON ORGANIZER*

PART 1 *INTO* THE LESSON

TIME REQUIRED	INSTRUCTIONAL ACTIVITIES	STUDENT PRODUCTS/CULMINATING TASKS

PART 2 *THROUGH* THE LESSON

TIME REQUIRED **DIRECTED(D) GUIDED(G) INDEPENDENT(I)** (LABEL EACH ACTIVITY)	INSTRUCTIONAL ACTIVITIES	STUDENT PRODUCTS/CULMINATING TASKS

ENGLISH FOR YOUR SUCCESS *LESSON ORGANIZER*

PART 3 *BEYOND* THE LESSON

CURRICULUM OR ENRICHMENT AREA (LIST)	ACTIVITY

🎴 African American Language, in itself, does not hinder learning. The method of teaching MAE is the main prohibitor.

CHAPTER 9

IMPLEMENTATION ISSUES

In 1979, the National Council of Teachers of English (NCTE) researched why speakers of African American Language did not fare well in America's educational institutions. Their findings revealed that AAL, in itself, did not hinder learning.

NCTE found that teachers adamantly embraced teaching methods that did not work. Rather than throw away their faulty methods, teachers tended to throw away their students with language differences.

NCTE found that teachers harbored negative attitudes about AAL. Negative attitudes exist not just on the part of educators, but in African Americans who have been programmed the same way. Many of us avoid acknowledging AAL as our first language. Because society disparages AAL, we tend to use it only among ourselves. As a result, persons outside the African American community, including teachers, tend to believe that we have corrected into mainstream English.

Most educators know little about the language, culture, and history of African Americans. They employ ineffective techniques for teaching language skills, and they refuse to adapt their teaching styles to meet the needs of all students. We are so boxed into what we are programmed to believe is good teaching, that when reality confronts us with a child who linguistically, behaviorally, and culturally differs from the prototype, we are lost. Sometimes we rationalize our use of the same methodologies by adopting the belief that speakers of AAL cannot learn. But if we seek what is best for children, we may need to change our instructional approach to fit the need profile of the children in front of us.

In order to effectively implement this program, teachers need to develop an understanding of second-language acquisition and an appreciation for cultural diversity. The implications of these two issues for program implementation are discussed below, along with strategies for providing effective models of MAE and AAL.

SECOND-LANGUAGE ACQUISITION

Steven Krashen, a prominent theorist in second-language acquisition, says all a person needs to learn a second language is comprehensible input in the new language. Krashen says affective filters such as anxiety, lack of confidence, poor self-esteem, and inadequate motivation can block this process. To the greatest practical extent, teachers must take steps to lower these filters.

First, a teacher must ensure the classroom is free from anxiety. Teachers should set up classrooms that comfortably engage children in interactive communication. Children should work in cooperative groups in their natural language. Teachers should talk less. Small group interaction could help introduce students to MAE and AAL through literature.

Teachers also must help to nurture and maintain students' self-esteem and confidence. One of the fastest ways to raise a child's affective filter is through correction. Evelyn Dandy, in her book, *Black Communication*, describes the true story of a young African American male who sat in a high reading group. On his turn in the reading circle, he eagerly began to read. While reading, he encountered the word *street*. When he said *screet*, the teacher interrupted him. "*Street*," she said. The boy read on and again encountered the word *street*. Again, he said *screet*. The teacher kept drilling him until finally the boy said he did not want to read anymore.

The teacher made this child feel he had a problem when, in fact, he did not. It was embarrassing and hurtful. As a result the teacher turned the child off to reading. When motivation to speak in class diminishes, learning suffers. As this book has shown, effective strategies are available to teachers for helping African American students acquire fluency in MAE—strategies that reflect knowledge of and respect for AAL.

⚘ Los Angeles pupils interact with each other in a variety of learning modes.

CULTURAL DIVERSITY

Before introducing strategies for helping students to master MAE, educators must begin with an appreciation of cultural diversity. In Los Angeles, when a school opts to enter the *Language Development Program for African American Students*, all teachers and para-educators must attend three full days of educational seminars—one day on language, one on culture, and the third on children's learning styles. These seminars are followed by a variety of staff development and training activities.

Teachers receive comprehensive training in literacy acquisition, language acquisition, learning styles, and identifying and bridging the strengths of these students toward academic success.

Teachers undergo continual development at and away from the school site. Training takes place during the regular workday and on weekends and other non-workdays. Also, the program gives teachers an opportunity to observe and discuss demonstration lessons.

Most participating teachers begin their school year by familiarizing children with the diversity of the world. Instruction treats diversity as a positive attribute. Teachers in our cultural seminars learn how to infuse African culture into the curriculum. This helps to improve the confidence and comfort of African American students, and thereby opens these students to becoming bicultural and bilingual.

Instructional units are offered on various populations and languages. For example, some second graders have performed a skit on the Italian book, *Strega Nona*. The teacher required the African American students to understand the nuances of Italian. The desirability of diversity must be established before teachers can begin the process of talking about AAL. It may require that educators build their understanding of the children in front of them in order to move smoothly through a diversity unit.

As part of the study of AAL, students are introduced to the sounds of indigenous African languages and they are given a sense of the history of their language. Students are introduced to literature written in AAL. In *English for Your Success*, each teacher must have a classroom library that reflects the culture of the children. Children love books that present them in a positive light.

MODELS OF MAE AND AAL

One key ingredient to a natural language learning environment is a model that speaks the target form. If our objective is to facilitate mastery of MAE, then we must provide a model in the classroom who speaks this language. Students would benefit further if the English model also has facility in students' home language(s). For example, an American classroom that enrolls Japanese-speaking children would provide the greatest educational benefit if the teacher were fluent in both English and Japanese.

The same holds for AAL. I had an advantage when I taught third grade because my facility with mainstream structure and AAL structure could help my students—most of whom were African American—master mainstream English.

Because students must be engaged to intuit the rule system, the classroom should include individuals who can model the target language form. Sometimes cooperative groupings will work. It has been estimated that about 15 percent of African Americans learn mainstream English first. Students from this group could serve as model speakers of mainstream English. Table groupings will facilitate interactive dialogue if they include model speakers.

In cases where teachers possess different linguistic strengths—for example, one is fluent in mainstream English and the other is fluent in AAL, these teachers could become more effective educators through team teaching.

In addition, para-educators who speak the language of the children can assist teachers in the classroom. These para-educators should receive training along with teachers, administrators, and parents.

🎗There are some often-asked questions about English for Your Success. The answers may help you to educate your school community as you implement EYS.

Chapter 10

Questions That Teachers, Parents, and Administrators Ask about The Program

What is the Program? What is African American Language?

Q: What is the primary goal of this program?

A: The program seeks to insure equity in access for African American students to the core curriculum, to post-secondary educational opportunities, and to career options by facilitating their acquisition of the primary language of instruction in American schools—Mainstream American English.

Q: What is African American Language (AAL)? How can I learn more about the rules governing AAL?

A: AAL, simply put, is a rule-governed, linguistic system that lays English lexicon (vocabulary) against an African rule system. Researchers who have done work on the rules governing AAL include Walt Wolfram, James Dillard, Lorenzo Turner, and Ronald Williams. (See the appendix (p. 00 for specific references.)

Q: How does AAL differ from mainstream English? Why is it important to distinguish between AAL and MAE?

A: AAL differs from mainstream English phonologically (in how sounds are used to construct words), morphosyntactically (in how words and sentences are formed to carry meaning), and pragmatically (in how language is used in social contexts). Failure to distinguish between the two language forms can short circuit communication between teachers whose primary

language is MAE and students whose primary language is AAL, and thereby deprive the child of an effective education.

Q: Our ancestry is American, not African. We go back six generations in America. Why do you teach my child about Africa as his/her ancestry?

A: While America has been home to African Americans for many generations, African cultural and linguistic patterns continue to pervade all aspects of their lives. Therefore, through understanding their ancestry, African American children can better understand who they are, where they have been, and where they are going.

※ By attending educational seminars, teachers learn the appropriate strategies to facilitate mainstream English mastery.

HOW DO TEACHERS IMPLEMENT THE PROGRAM?

Q: How can I make sure I am implementing the program properly?

A: Teachers should participate in educational seminars and collaboratives that emphasize appropriate instructional strategies that facilitate mainstream English mastery. Areas in which teachers should seek knowledge and expertise include:

❦ instructional methods for teaching MAE as a second language;

❦ infusing the history and culture of the target population into the curriculum; and

❦ using technology as a tool for facilitating language acquisition. In addition, teachers must come to accept, accommodate, and affirm the strengths and learning styles of all their students.

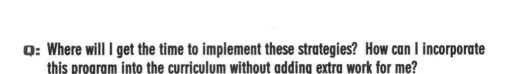

Q: Where will I get the time to implement these strategies? How can I incorporate this program into the curriculum without adding extra work for me?

A: The good news is that this program is not a new curriculum, but rather a collection of linguistically appropriate and culturally consistent instructional strategies that can be infused into existing curriculum without requiring additional time.

Q: How can teachers effectively integrate this program into daily classroom activities, given all the other subjects we need to teach?

A: The program encourages teachers to replace ineffective approaches with a continuum of language arts strategies that research shows are more effective for moving African American students toward English language proficiency. Thus no additional time should be required.

Q: How does this program tie in to science, math, and other courses?

A: Language is the basis for all academic learning. Students who lack proficiency in the language of instruction will be unable to thrive in science, math, and other subjects.

Q: Why is it important for teachers to understand the language of the African American child in order to effectively teach him/her?

A: Learning requires communication between the teacher and the student. If the teacher does not understand the primary language of the student, effective education will not occur.

Q: I didn't grow up around Black people, so I am unfamiliar with AAL. How can I help students whose primary language is AAL?

A: Proficiency in AAL is not a requirement for teaching MAE to African American students. However, the more familiar you become with the culture and the characteristic features of the language of African American students, the better able you will be to teach the target language (MAE).

Q: What is the best way to describe the program to parents?

A: First inform parents in straightforward language that the goal of the program is to help their youngster master the language of instruction. Also let parents know that the program's instructional strategies are research-based and that the program provides training to help parents support their child's development of proficiency in the language of instruction.

Q: Does each teacher have the flexibility to decide which materials he/she should use?

A: Yes. Teachers have flexibility in selecting culturally appropriate materials.

Q: Will training and support be needed for teachers?

A: Yes. Teachers will need ongoing training in culturally relevant teaching techniques and effective methodologies for helping African American students master mainstream English.

Q: How do I implement this program in a classroom that has students who are not all speakers of AAL?

A: The program employs several strategies in classrooms that enroll diverse student populations. In some instances two or more teachers form a team—one teacher works with African-American students while other teachers work with other students. In single-teacher classrooms, teachers provide instruction in ways that reflect the diversity of the students' language backgrounds. For example, students may be organized into cooperative groups based on language usage—while some lessons may require single-language groupings, other lessons may require mixed language groupings.

Q: How does the program relate to special education?

A: While the program was not designed for special education, its instructional strategies may be employed by special education teachers who work with African American students.

Q: All my students speak MAE; why do I need the program?

A: In this case the primary goal of the program will have been achieved. However, students might yet benefit from other components of the program such as cultural infusion and bridging the learning styles of African American students. More generally, the program could help prepare educators to teach African American students who enter their classrooms in future years.

WHAT IMPACT DOES THE PROGRAM HAVE ON STUDENT ACHIEVEMENT?

Q: What evidence is there that this is an effective approach to teaching MAE?

A: Many studies have shown that instructional strategies that take into account the home language of African American students are more effective for moving these students toward mastery of mainstream English. For example, H. Taylor (***Standard English, Black English, and Bidialectalism***, 1991) conducted an experiment to assess the relative impact of contrastive analysis on student learning. One group of students (the experimental group) used contrastive analysis to highlight the differences between AAL and mainstream English, while a second group (the control group) followed "traditional English" techniques. After eleven weeks, the experimental group showed a 59 percent reduction in occurrences in AAL features in their mainstream English writing, while the control group actually showed a slight increase (8.5 percent) of occurrences of AAL in their mainstream English writing. Other studies have shown similar effects for the instructional strategies used in our program.

The school environment must be receptive to African American culture.

Q: How do I know this program is working in my classroom?

A: You know the program is working when students progress steadily toward mastery of MAE in its oral and written forms as documented in student work (for example, written language journals and oral language activities).

Q: How will this program improve or strengthen our readers?

A: Language acquisition is a prerequisite for reading. Thus, the greater facility students have with MAE in its oral form, the better they will be able to read in this language.

✤ Practicing MAE in its oral form improves and strengthens students' reading skills.

Q: When will we see results of improvement in our children's language?

A: Beginning the first year of implementation teachers should begin to see movement toward proficiency in the use of mainstream English structures. However, language acquisition occurs over an extended period of time. Research indicates that complete mastery may take from five to seven years.

WHY SHOULD MY CHILD PARTICIPATE IN THIS PROGRAM?

Q: Will this program benefit my child in ways other than mastery of MAE?

A: Yes. The program will also provide children with an awareness and appreciation of different cultures and languages.

Q: Will this approach carry over to the next grade?

A: Yes. By design, the program should be implemented as a continuum across all elementary and secondary grades.

Q: I want my child to know mainstream English and to be in a rigorous classroom on grade level. Is this it?

A: Yes. This program challenges teachers to implement a rigorous instructional curriculum.

Q: Will learning to speak correctly help my child learn in all academic areas?

A: Yes. Language provides access to learning in all academic areas. Functional skills in oral and written forms of MAE facilitate success in social studies, math, science, and other subjects.

Q: Will this program enhance my child's ability to be a successful test taker?

A: Yes. Tests are language-based.

❀ Parents can help their children by taking courses to improve their own proficiency in English.

WHAT CAN PARENTS DO TO HELP THEIR CHILDREN?

Q: How can I help my child become proficient in MAE?

A: Parents can help their children become proficient in English by taking courses to improve their own proficiency in English, by reading to their children, and by creating an interactive language-rich home environment where children are engaged in oral and written communications and are provided the opportunity to observe parents engaged in similar activities.

Q: I speak AAL. How can I help my child's language development?

A: Parents whose primary language is AAL can acquire proficiency in mainstream English so that they can serve as a language model for their children. Parents can engage their children in listening, speaking, and writing activities on a daily basis.

Q: Will this program try to correct my child's way of speaking?

A: This program adds a new language to the child's linguistic repertoire. As a result, the child is able to communicate in different cultural environments.

WHAT DO SCHOOL ADMINISTRATORS NEED TO KNOW AND DO TO IMPLEMENT THE PROGRAM?

Q: How can I help to support and implement this program?

A: Principals are critical to the successful implementation of school-level programs. To support this program, principals should:

ꝗ familiarize themselves with the program;

ꝗ provide opportunities for professional development and training;

ꝗ encourage teachers to apply the program's strategies; and

ꝗ involve parents as partners in classroom and school activities related to language acquisition.

Q: Will it take the whole school and every faculty member to agree to make this program work?

A: Complete buy-in by the entire faculty gives the program a better chance of being fully and effectively implemented.

Q: Does the program require training for administrators?

A: Yes. In order to be effective, school administrators need to internalize the basic philosophy and implementation strategies of the program. Therefore, training is critical for school administrators who are responsible for overseeing the implementation of the program.

Q: Does the program require teachers to be away from the class?

A: Teachers are required to participate in a variety of staff development activities. To the greatest possible extent,

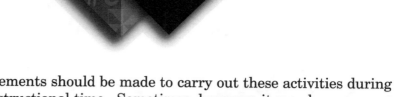

arrangements should be made to carry out these activities during non-instructional time. Sometimes, however, it may be necessary for teachers to be away from their classrooms in order to participate in staff development activities.

Q: How long will it take before the school fully implements the program?

A: On the average it takes about a year to reach full implementation (that is, gather instructional materials, create a print-rich, language-learning environment, and provide teachers with a sufficient knowledge base in the program's philosophy and instructional strategies).

Q: Will there be time set aside for sharing information and ideas?

A: Teachers are encouraged to form ongoing critical friends groups in order to share information, ideas, and experiences.

Q: Will this program cost additional money? How much?

A: Additional funds may be needed to provide the instructional tools and equipment such as listening centers, computers, electronic dictionaries and thesauruses, overhead projectors, television/VCR. Funds are also needed to release teachers for staff development and/or to compensate for additional work or training. The amount needed depends on the number of children, number of teachers, and the availability of existing resources.

EYS/LDPAAS Exemplary Classrooms
A Model of Classroom Implementation

At its core, the **English For Your Success** (EYS) or **Language Development Program for African American Students** (LDPAAS) is about effective instructional practices and classroom interventions that make a difference for students acquiring mainstream English as a second language so that they experience academic success. Ultimately, the program seeks to create classroom environments that facilitate language learning and literacy acquisition. The exemplary **LDPAAS** classroom can be viewed as having three critical components: a model environment, an exemplary teacher, and successful students.

Model Environment

The **EYS/LDPAAS** model classroom environment stimulates language development and literacy acquisition by surrounding students with a language rich environment rife with symbols and print. The process is akin to the way that oral language in infants is stimulated by a vigorous language environment in the home. In addition, the arranged environment creates the spatial context in which movement and learning activities takes place. At a minimum, there should be evidence of:

_____ A print-rich classroom environment at children's eye level

_____ An arranged environment that facilitates collaborative and interactive learning

_____ Writing Centers that include writing prompts, reader response and other writing journals, computers and word processing software

_____ Oral Language Centers featuring listening centers with headphones and stories on audiocassette (both commercially produced and featuring the voices of the students and teacher)

_____ Cultural art and community materials on display to establish a familiar context

_____ Classroom libraries, book nooks, reading corners, and books on display everywhere, within reach and accessible

_____ Reference materials where they are needed (dictionaries, encyclopedias, word lists, alphabet cards, calendars, magazines, telephone books, newspapers, maps, pictures, both print and electronic thesauruses, etc.)

_____ Recording materials and tools everywhere

_____ A variety of work spaces for students to settle into for reading and writing (in addition to students' desks)

_____ Adequate surrounding space for desks, bookcases, tables, etc.

_____ Functional print in view to direct daily routines like lunch count, center sign-ups, homework turned in, etc.

_____ Multimedia and technology utilized as instructional tools throughout the day (overhead projectors, computers and printers, **_LDPAAS_** developed and other recommended software)

_____ Clean, organized, and functional classroom environment

EXEMPLARY TEACHER

The **_EYS_** or **_LDPAAS_** Exemplary Teacher represents the very best in program implementation. S/he is well grounded in the program's rationale, philosophy, instructional methodologies, goals, and objectives. Utilization of the physical and emotional environment that s/he creates, and the daily instruction that s/he delivers, reflect positively on her or himself, the school, and the teaching profession in general. The **_EFYS/LDPAAS_** Exemplary Teacher:

_____ Accepts, accommodates, and affirms diversity

_____ Allows students to experience African American and mainstream cultures through literature, music, history, art and customs

_____ Infuses recommended strategies and approaches into their instructional delivery including SDAIE, contrastive analysis, language and language experience, collaborative and cooperative learning, and a balanced approach to literacy

_____ Employs multiple modality teaching techniques into instruction

_____ Provides opportunities for students consistent exposure to and interaction with MAE

_____ Maintains student outcomes in student and classroom portfolios

_____ Actively participates in all school-site staff development activities

_____ Attends the annual **LDPAAS** Staff Development Conference

_____ Engages in parental involvement activities to develop Parents as Partners in the educational process

_____ Articulates the **LDPAAS** philosophy with ease, confidence, and strong conviction

SUCCESSFUL STUDENTS

Successful students in the **EYS\LDPAAS** classroom are firmly grounded in their home language and culture while at the same time acquiring fluency in, and an understanding of, the language and culture of others. As students progress through the grade levels, they reflect an increased mastery of MAE, enabling them to communicate effectively in cross cultural environments and experience mastery of the subject matter and academic success. In the classroom, one would find the students:

_____ Engaged with materials and in activities that increase the students' understanding and awareness of African American culture and language structures

_____ Working collaboratively with peers and the teacher to produce projects and reports, and engaging in instructional conversations that provide a model of the target language

_____ Engaged in frequent opportunities to explore multiple discourse patterns and styles in MAE through literature, narratives, poetry, folktales, etc.

_____ Acquiring skills within context of activities that encourage listening, speaking, reading, writing and thinking

_____ Demonstrating/displaying increased mastery of MAE in its oral and written form

IMPLEMENTATION GUIDES AND CHECKLISTS

Four guides/checklists are provided in this section that have been developed to assist schools in implementing *English for Your Success.* The first guide helps teachers implement each of the program's 12 student goals. For each student goal, the guide delineates what students will be able to do, recommends approaches for reaching the goal, identifies selected strategies for implementing the approaches, and provides examples of student work products. The second guide provides a checklist of the characteristics of exemplary classroom teachers. The third guide enumerates the role of school facilitators in implementing the program. The fourth and final guide lists the characteristics of a model demonstration teacher.

TEACHER GUIDES FOR STUDENT GOALS

GOAL 1: Develop an appreciation of/for the language and culture of the home.

STUDENTS WILL BE ABLE TO:

Listen, write, and talk about self, family, neighborhood, and culture

Listen, write, and talk about African-American literature

Identify culturally relevant aspects of art, posters and artifacts

Conduct research (locate, observe/gather, analyze, and conclude)

RECOMMENDED APPROACHES FOR REACHING GOAL:

Infuse student's history and culture into the curriculum

Create a classroom environment that helps students recognize, respect, and appreciate their own language and culture

Incorporate parental and community support in the educational process

Use literature that reflects students' home life, personal interests, cultural background, and language

POSSIBLE STRATEGIES FOR IMPLEMENTING RECOMMENDED APPROACHES:

Cultural centers and classroom libraries that feature art and artifacts, games, costumes, clothing, posters, pictorial histories, etc.

Students develop a family tree and family quilts, interview parents or grandparents, and visit community sites and organizations

Use African-American poetry, short stories, and novels in literature lessons

Read culturally appropriate magazines and newspapers that feature a range of reading levels and a variety of topics

POSSIBLE STUDENT PRODUCTS:

Audio-taped and videotaped recitations of memorized poems, songs, and chants

Culturally relevant artwork

Oral and written reports on self, family, and the neighborhood, including classroom visitations by parents, grandparents, and community members

Songs, chants, and poems

GOAL 2: Develop receptive language in Mainstream American English (MAE).

STUDENTS WILL BE ABLE TO:

Read, write, speak, and listen for many purposes

Communicate with legible and complete sentences

Listen to, read, and understand simple MAE words and sentences

Use multiple media to express ideas in MAE

RECOMMENDED APPROACHES FOR REACHING GOAL:

Use total modality teaching techniques in the classroom

Conduct instructional conversations in MAE to: (a) encourage student-to-student and teacher-to-student interaction in collaborative learning contexts; and (b) provide a model of the target language

Engage students in authentic learning activities incorporating materials that are aligned with their interests

Emphasize vocabulary development with a focus on synonyms

Provide opportunities for continual exposure to the target language through literature

Emphasize learning activities that allow students to hear the target language (MAE)

POSSIBLE STUDENT PRODUCTS:

Journal of written and oral responses to literature

Essays or book report using a computer word processor

Personal dictionaries and thesauruses

Audio-taped and videotaped recitations

Thematic projects that involve use of MAE

POSSIBLE STRATEGIES FOR IMPLEMENTING RECOMMENDED APPROACHES:

Student participation in activities that are hands-on

Use of collaborative groups, including peer tutoring and editing

Daily engagement of students in writing process

Matching students' personal interests and abilities to materials

Providing authentic learning opportunities

Encouraging vocabulary development through communication

Reading every day

Student infusion of multimedia resources

GOAL 3: Acquire basic literary skills.

STUDENTS WILL BE ABLE TO:

Write, speak, and listen for many purposes

Use the writing process

Discuss and report ideas, thoughts, and feelings about literature

Select books for free voluntary reading

RECOMMENDED APPROACHES FOR REACHING GOAL:

Incorporate a balanced literacy approach using material from African-American culture

Create a print-rich classroom that includes teacher and student-generated lists, newspapers, maps, charts, magazines, resources, books, and a classroom library that reflects students' home language and culture

Emphasize small group activities to encourage language development and the sharing of ideas

Provide students with daily opportunities to read and be read to in their school and home environment

Use technology as a tool in language and literacy acquisition

Integrate oral and written language into all curricular areas

POSSIBLE STUDENT PRODUCTS:

Student-authored projects (books, poems, magazines)

Audio-taped readings and responses to literature

Videotaped readings, responses, and interpretations of literature

Dramatizations and debates

POSSIBLE STRATEGIES FOR IMPLEMENTING RECOMMENDED APPROACHES:

Reading and writing using authentic materials that facilitate communication

Reading and writing learned through experience

Skill lessons done in context

Display of printed material

Collaborative groups with equitable sharing of tasks

Silent-sustained reading time with student-selected texts

Reading centers or corners and author chairs

Use of technology—listening center (audio books), TV/VCR, computer, etc.

Journal writing

Thematic integration with other subject areas

GOAL 4: Develop an awareness and appreciation of diversity.

STUDENTS WILL BE ABLE TO:

Read, write, speak, and listen in multiple language and cultural contexts

Identify and understand elements and characteristics of other cultures

Compare the elements of African-American culture with elements of the mainstream and other cultures

Discuss cultural issues in a structured, collaborative setting

RECOMMENDED APPROACHES FOR REACHING GOAL:

Use the various languages and cultures represented in the school and classroom to help students appreciate diversity

Use multicultural artifacts, literature, arts, crafts, music, and holidays to facilitate awareness and appreciation of diversity

Provide opportunities for students to explore the uniqueness of their culture and to identify and respect similarities and differences in other cultures

Explore various cultures in order to assist students in interacting effectively in different cultural contexts

POSSIBLE STRATEGIES FOR IMPLEMENTING RECOMMENDED APPROACHES:

Recognizing and acknowledging all children in the classroom

Openly discussing different languages and cultures

Involving students, parents, family members, faculty, staff, and other school visitors in a collaborative study of cultures

Providing students with access to artifacts, arts, and crafts

Exposing students to music and literature from around the world

Exploring the achievements and contributions of different cultures through instruction in the core academic subjects

Comparing different cultures and languages represented in the classroom

Analyzing how the African-American experience compares with that of the mainstream culture and other cultures around the world

Analyzing the language requirements of different situations and social contexts

POSSIBLE STUDENT PRODUCTS:

Multicultural representations and projects

Video-taped role-playing

Essays

Poems

Costumes

Puppet shows

Surveys

GOAL 5: Recognize and label the differences between African American Language (AAL) and Mainstream American English (MAE).

STUDENTS WILL BE ABLE TO:

Recognize major linguistic differences between AAL and MAE

Identify selected linguistic features and characteristics of AAL

Switch between AAL and MAE

RECOMMENDED APPROACHES FOR REACHING GOALS:

Compare the oral and written components of different languages

Use teachable moments during content instruction to identify and explain language differences

Use the editing phase of writing to examine differences between AAL and MAE

POSSIBLE STRATEGIES FOR IMPLEMENTING RECOMMENDED APPROACHES:

Using contrastive analysis within content lessons to reinforce the target concepts

Using the editing phase of the writing process to encourage students to translate between AAL and MAE

POSSIBLE STUDENT PRODUCTS:

Video-taped situational role-playing

Games

Written translations

Audio taping

Songs/sounds

GOAL 6: Expand personal thesaurus of conceptually coded word concepts.

STUDENTS WILL BE ABLE TO:

Read, write, speak, and listen for a variety of purposes using expanded vocabulary

Define words within the context of their use

Identify, understand, and use synonyms, antonyms, and homonyms

RECOMMENDED APPROACHES FOR REACHING GOAL:

Provide opportunities for multiple exposure to MAE discourse style

Focus on vocabulary development with an emphasis on synonyms, antonyms, prefixes, and suffixes

Motivate students to appreciate literature and the role it plays in developing personal vocabularies

POSSIBLE STRATEGIES FOR IMPLEMENTING RECOMMENDED APPROACHES:

Reciting speeches, debating issues, and reading scripts

Role-playing

Vocabulary development centered around actual events and students lives

Contextual vocabulary development balanced with dictionary use

POSSIBLE STUDENT PRODUCTS:

Video-taped role-playing

Books (audio and written)

Translations (for example, rap songs to MAE)

Personal thesauruses

Puzzles

Skits

GOAL 7: Analyze linguistic differences between African American Language (AAL) and Mainstream American English (MAE).

STUDENTS WILL BE ABLE TO:

Read, write, speak, and listen for a variety of purposes

Analyze linguistic differences between AAL and MAE in particular contexts (contrastive analysis)

Talk and write about differences between AAL and MAE

RECOMMENDED APPROACHES FOR REACHING GOAL:

Use a variety of literary works to compare and contrast the linguistic features of AAL and MAE

Use samples of students' daily oral and written language to compare and contrast AAL and MAE

POSSIBLE STRATEGIES FOR IMPLEMENTING RECOMMENDED APPROACHES:

Read six to ten literature titles that are culturally and linguistically relevant to students because they feature African and African-American people, culture, and language

Employ contrastive analysis

Validate students' oral and written language in a positive, affirming classroom environment

POSSIBLE STUDENT PRODUCTS:

Letters

Reports

Video-taped skits

Demonstrations

Opinion pieces

Pamphlets

GOAL 8: Use Mainstream American English (MAE) structure functionally in oral and written form.

STUDENTS WILL BE ABLE TO:

Read, write, speak, and listen for a variety of purposes

Give an oral report

Contribute good ideas in small and large group discussion

Formulate, express, and support opinions

Use and internalize the writing process

RECOMMENDED APPROACHES FOR REACHING GOAL:

Use oral language activities to promote the development of MAE

Use written language activities to promote the development of MAE

Provide opportunities to compare and practice oral and written MAE discourse patterns

POSSIBLE STRATEGIES FOR IMPLEMENTING RECOMMENDED APPROACHES:

Reciting speeches, participating in debates, and holding moot court and mock trials

Participation in plays and theater productions that feature MAE

Role-play situations that require MAE

Daily writing activities

Preparation of writing portfolios

POSSIBLE STUDENT PRODUCTS:

Monologues

Dialogues

Oratorical contests

Letters

Journals

GOAL 9: Recognize the language requirements of different situations.

STUDENTS WILL BE ABLE TO:

Read, write, speak, and listen for a variety of purposes

Identify language requirements for a particular situation

Use the appropriate language for the appropriate situation

Communicate ideas and feelings in different language situations

Switch language codes and justify reason for switching

RECOMMENDED APPROACHES FOR REACHING GOAL:

Use a variety of situations for students to judge and select language for effective communication

Introduce students to oral communication patterns of AAL and MAE and provide opportunities for their use

Provide opportunities for students to observe MAE models outside of the classroom environment

POSSIBLE STRATEGIES FOR IMPLEMENTING RECOMMENDED APPROACHES:

Role-playing in real and imagined situations that require the use of both AAL and MAE

Placing equal value on AAL and MAE

School journeys, including field trips and classroom visits by experts

Career days

POSSIBLE STUDENT PRODUCTS:

Dramatizations

Audio-taped classroom discussions

Skits

Video presentations

Graphs

Travel brochures

GOAL 10: Demonstrate proficient use of MAE in oral and written form.

STUDENTS WILL BE ABLE TO:

Write and speak for specific audiences using MAE

Fully and clearly develop central ideas for writing and speaking

Write and speak using MAE mechanics, diction, usage, and sentence structure

RECOMMENDED APPROACHES FOR REACHING GOAL:

Use a variety of writing documents for students to demonstrate continued mastery in MAE

Offer students formal and informal opportunities to demonstrate oral mastery of MAE

STUDENTS WILL BE ABLE TO:

Engage in daily, weekly, and monthly writing activities

Form collaborative groups to discuss issues and key concepts

Employ technology as a tool

POSSIBLE STUDENT PRODUCTS:

Advertisements

Stories

Diaries

Oral defenses

Oral reports

Electronic medium productions

News stories

GOAL 11: Demonstrate an expanded knowledge and appreciation of the language and culture of the home of others.

STUDENTS WILL BE ABLE TO:

Read, write, speak, and listen for a variety of purposes

Describe differences and similarities between and among cultures

Discuss issues and ideas about different cultures

Identify traits of own culture and compare with other cultures

RECOMMENDED APPROACHES FOR REACHING GOAL:

Examine the similarities and differences within the primary culture

Examine the similarities and differences among cultures

Create a school and classroom environment that respects multiculturalism

POSSIBLE STRATEGIES FOR IMPLEMENTING RECOMMENDED APPROACHES:

Employing old and contemporary views of culture

Examining culture across a historical continuum through the present

Studying other cultures in the context of other content areas

Sponsoring cultural days for the cultures represented at the school

POSSIBLE STUDENT PRODUCTS:

Costumes

Clothing

Cultural art

Writing samples

Video and audio tapes

Internet correspondences

Cultural web pages

GOAL 12: Communicate effectively in cross-cultural environments.

STUDENTS WILL BE ABLE TO:

Read, write, and speak for a variety of purposes

Determine meanings of text in a variety of language situations

Produce quality examples of persuasive, informative, and entertaining writing

Develop a position on an issue and debate it effectively

Identify the purpose of specific communications

RECOMMENDED APPROACHES FOR REACHING GOAL:

Use real situations to examine communicative effectiveness in different cultural contexts

POSSIBLE STRATEGIES FOR IMPLEMENTING RECOMMENDED APPROACHES:

School-to-work programs

Volunteer work

Writing articles for newspapers

Presentation to the board of education

POSSIBLE STUDENT PRODUCTS:

Research/term papers

End of unit/term projects

Radio/television program

Newspaper

On-line discussions

TEACHER AND FACILITATOR GUIDE

EXEMPLARY CLASSROOM TEACHER GUIDE

AN EXEMPLARY CLASSROOM TEACHER:

Continually demonstrates a strong grasp of the program's rationale, philosophy, goals and objectives

Actively participates in the program's educational seminars:

▲ Language Acquisition for African American Students

▲ Literacy & Learning: Building on Learning Styles and Strengths

▲ Cultural Grounding

Infuses seminar concepts into structured lesson plans

Includes lesson outcomes in student portfolios

IN ORDER TO GROUND STUDENTS CULTURALLY, AN EXEMPLARY CLASSROOM TEACHER:

Accepts, affirms, and accommodates diversity

Defines African American and Mainstream American English (MAE) cultures through daily instruction

Allows students to experience African American and MAE cultures through literature, language, music, history, art, and customs

Teaches the values of multiculturalism

TO SUPPORT SCHOOL-WIDE IMPLEMENTATION OF THE PROGRAM, AN EXEMPLARY CLASSROOM TEACHER:

Actively participates in ALL school site staff development activities

Facilitates the involvement of Parents as Partners in student learning

Articulates the program's goals and strategies with ease, confidence and conviction

Attends the annual staff development conference put on by the *Language Development Program for African American Students*

AN EXEMPLARY CLASSROOM TEACHER MAINTAINS AND EFFECTIVELY USES A MODEL CLASSROOM THAT FEATURES:

A "culturally validating environment" containing:

- ▲ Culturally representative art, artifacts, posters, etc.

- ▲ African arts & crafts (including kits and activities)

- ▲ African history and culture (e.g., Kwanzaa) on video and audio

Culturally relevant classroom library and reading centers

- ▲ Literature (history/profiles of African Americans and other cultures)

- ▲ Supplementary texts (Africa/African American History, Science, etc.)

Oral language centers

- ▲ Stories on cassette

- ▲ Tape players/recorders

- ▲ Listening center set with headphones

- ▲ Mini-filmstrip projector and props for dramatization

Writing Centers

- ▲ Dictionaries (books and electronic, i.e., *Language Masters*)

- ▲ Thesauruses (Grades 2-8)

- ▲ Writing prompts

- ▲ Writing journals for daily entries

- ▲ Reading response journals

- ▲ Computers with appropriate software

Multimedia & technology as tools of instruction

- ▲ Daily use of the overhead projector

- ▲ Computer(s), printer(s), and appropriate software

ROLE OF THE SCHOOL SITE FACILITATOR:

Coordinate relationships between district headquarters and the school site

Work closely with site administrators to facilitate program implementation

Share effective program strategies with teachers—implementing MESL (mainstream English as a second language) strategies, using technology in the classroom, setting up classrooms that nurture literacy

Recommend, order, log, inventory and distribute instructional materials

Assess the instructional/material needs of teachers

Coordinate staff development sessions based on identified needs

Work with a Parent Representative to set up and maintain a Parent Information Center and Parent Workshops

Inform parents and community of program activities, update teachers and paraprofessionals on seminars and other activities and display student work

Set up a program reference library for use by your staff

A MODEL DEMONSTRATION TEACHER FOR THIS PROGRAM:

Understands and demonstrates "SDAIE" strategies

Understands and demonstrates "Contrastive Analysis" strategies

Understands and implements an integrated reading/language arts program (listening, speaking, reading, writing) that includes daily reading to students

Includes "whole language" strategies in instruction

Has knowledge of and infuses students' history and culture into instruction

Orients students toward the appropriate uses of language in various formal and informal situations

Effectively employs heterogeneous cooperative learning groups in the classroom

Incorporates students' written language journals into daily instruction

Employs multiple modalities in teaching program concepts

Provides students with opportunities for consistent exposure to and use of Mainstream American English

Provides a block of time for teaching mainstream English as a second language (MESL), language breaks, or mainstream English mastery (MEM) teaming

Builds instruction around authentic, student-directed learning

AFRICAN AND AFRICAN AMERICAN LITERATURE

**LOS ANGELES UNIFIED SCHOOL DISTRICT
DIVISION OF INSTRUCTION
Language Development Program for
African American Students
African and African American Literature
for Grades K-8**

AFRICAN LITERATURE

a is For Africa, Owoo
A trip through the alphabet using terms from the African continent.
Ages 4-6, Grade levels K-1

Africa: Brothers and Sisters, Kroll, Virginia
Little boy and his father travel to Africa and learn about its people and customs.
Ages 7-10, Grade levels 2-5
ISBN: 0027511669

Anansi Goes Fishing, Kimmell, Eric
Trickster Anansi the Spider is outwitted by his friend Turtle in a tale which explains the origin of spider webs.
Ages 5-9, Grade levels K-4
ISBN: 0-8234-0918X

Ashanti to Zulu, Musgrove, Margaret
Twenty-six African traditions are explained from A to Z.
Ages 9 and up, Grade levels 4 and up

Beat the Story Drum, Pum-Pum, Bryan, Ashley
Five traditional Nigerian tales told in rhythmic language and accompanied by bold woodcuts.
ISBN: 0-689-31356-X

Beneath the Rainbow, Gakuo, Kariuki
A collection of Children's stories and poems from Kenya.
Ages 6 -12, Grade levels 1-7
ISBN: 9966-884-60-2

Boy of the Pyramids, Jones, Ruth F.
A mystery of Ancient Egypt: Kaffe, born into a wealthy, Egyptian family is allowed to buy a slave; a little girl who becomes his playmate. Together they capture a robber who has been stealing jewels from one of the tombs of the Pharaohs.
Ages 10 -11, Grade levels 5-6

Chain of Fire, Naidoo, Beverly
For mature readers. Sequel to **Journey to Jo'burg**. When the villagers of Bophelong are forced to leave their homes and resettle, 15-year-old Naledi and her younger brother join in a school demonstration.
Ages 10 -11, Grade levels 5-6
ISBN: 0397324278

Count Your Way Through Africa, Haskins, Jim
Jim Haskins has written over 30 books for children, and in this new series he introduces children to foreign cultures.
Ages 6 -9, Grade levels 1-4
ISBN: 0-87614-347-8; 0-87614-514-4

A Country Far Away, Gray, Higel
Parallel pictures reveal the similarities in the lives of two boys, one in a western country and one in an African village.
Grade level Pre-K-1
ISBN: 0-531-08392-6

Cow-Tail Switch and Other West African Stories, Courlander, Harold
A collection of West African folk tales about men, animals, kings, warriors, and farmers.
ISBN: 0-8050-0288-X; 0-8050-0298-7

The Egyptian Cinderella, Climo, Shirley
In this version of Cinderella set in Egypt in the sixth century BC, Rhodopis, a slave girl, eventually comes to be chosen by the Pharaoh to be his queen.
ISBN: 0-690-04824-6

Fortune Tellers, Alexander, Lloyd
A young man finds fame and fortune through the advice of a fortune teller.
Grade level Pre-K-1
ISBN: 0-525-44849-7

The Great Greedy Orge, Cooper, Gail
The Elly Activity series developed for early learners teach basic concepts and language skills and promote hand-eye coordination.
Ages 3-6, Grade levels K-1,
ISBN: 9966-884-84-X

Hugo Hippo's ABC Coloring Book of Africa, Porter, Gail A.
This coloring book rendition of **Hugo Hippo's ABC Fun Book** in Africa provides children
with hours of coloring fun touring Africa with Hugo Hippo and his wildlife friends.
Ages 4-8, Grade levels Pre K-3,
ISBN: 9966-884-24-6

Hugo Hippo's ABC Fun Book in Africa, Porter, Gail A.
Features an alliterative test starring the lovable Hugo Hippo and a host of wildlife characters.
Ages 4 - 8, Grade levels Pre-K-3,
ISBN: 9966-884-36-X

Into the Mummy's Tomb, Reeves, Nicholas
An account of Howard Carter's discovery of the Tomb of King Tutankhamun, descriptions of the artifacts inside and their importance, the discovery in 1988 of more artifacts, and theories about the curse associated with the tomb are included.
Grade level 5-6
ISBN: 0-590-45752-7

Jambo Means Hello, Feelings, Muriel
A Caldecott Honor Book, Muriel and Tom Feelings wrote and illustrated this Swahili alphabet book.
 All ages, All grades
ISBN: 0-8037-4350-5

Journey to Jo'burg, Naidoo, Beverly
A South African story. When their baby sister becomes ill, 13-year-old Naledi and her younger brother make a journey of over 300 kilometers from their village to Johannesburg, where their mother works as a maid.
Ages 10-11, Grade levels 5-6
ISBN: 0-397-32168-8; 0-06-440237-1

Mara, Daughter of the Nile, Jarvis, Eloise
Mara, a proud and beautiful slave girl in ancient Egypt, risks her life for her freedom when she becomes a double agent for two enemies, Queen Hatshepsut and her young half-brother, as they vie for the throne.
Ages 10-11, Grade levels 5-6
ISBN: 0-8446-6536-3

Masai And I, Kroll, Virginia
Linda, a little girl who lives in the city, learns about East Africa and the Masai in school, and imagines what her life might be like if she were Masai.
Grade level 2-3
ISBN: 0-02-751165-0

Mecheshi Goes to the Game Park, Mbuja, Kioi
Mecheshi and her younger brother visit a game park with their uncle, the game ranger. Full color illustrations provide many wild animals to look at and talk about.
Ages 4-9, Grade levels Pre-K-4
ISBN: 9966-884-48-3

Mecheshi Goes to the Market, Mbuga, Kioi
It's market day, and Mecheshi goes with her mother to the market. She meets various traders and gets into all kinds of mischief.
Ages 4-9, Grade levels Pre K-4
ISBN: 9966-884-00-9

Mojo Means One, Feelings, Muriel
Handsomely illustrated book which teaches the Swahili words for the numbers 1-10 as well as providing information of East African culture.
Ages 4-10, Grade levels K-5,
ISBN: 0-8057-5777-8; 0-8037-5711-5

Mufaro's Beautiful Daughter, Steptoe, John
A young king seeking a wife comes upon Mufaro's two beautiful daughters and must choose the one worthy to be his bride.
Ages 6-8, Grade levels 1-3,
ISBN: 0-688-04046-2

Mummies Made in Egypt, Aliki
Describes the technique and the reasons for the use of mummification in Ancient Egypt.
ISBN: 0-690-03859-3

Ntombi's Song, Seed, Jenny
When a speeding bus causes her to spill the sugar she is carrying home, Ntombi, a six-year-old Zulu girl, is determined to overcome her fears and find a way to earn money to buy more sugar.
Ages 8-9, Grade levels 3-4
ISBN: 0-8070-8318-6

Nyalgondhio Wuod-Ombare and the Lost Woman from Lake Victoria, Oswaggo, Joel
A traditional Kenyan tale. This classic story from the Luo ethnic groups of Kenya is a tale of a fisherman by Lake Victoria who receives—and then squanders—his gifts from God.
Ages 9 and up, Grade levels 3 and up
ISBN: 9966-884-72-6

Nyumba Ya Mumbi, Gakuo, Kariuki
Set in the heart of Kenya, tells of the origins of the Kikuy clans and the blessing offered to them by Nagaum.
Ages 9 and up, Grade levels 3 and up
ISBN: 9966-884-12-2

Orphan Boy, Mollel, Tololwa
Although delighted by the orphan boy who has come into his life, an old man becomes very curious about the boy's mysterious powers.
Ages 5-8, Grade levels K-3
ISBN: 0-89919-985-2

Osa's Pride, Ann Grifalconi
Tale of an African girl who comes face to face with her vain nature and what she does to attempt to change herself.
Ages 5-8, Grade levels K-3,
ISBN: 0-316-32865-0

Over the Green Hills, Turner, Rachel Isadora
Zolani, who lives in a rural black homeland in South Africa, goes with his mother to visit his Grandma Zindzi.
Grade level Pre-K-2
ISBN: 0-688-1-510-6

Rehema's Journey, Margolis, Barbara
Rehema, a nine-year-old girl who lives in the mountains of Tanzania, accompanies her father to Arusha City and visits the Ngorongoro Crater.
Grade level 6-8
ISBN: 0-590-42846-2

Sahara, Reynolds, Jan
Describes the way of life of the Tuaregs, a nomadic culture that presently exists in the Sahara, the world's largest desert.
ISBN: 0-15-269959-7; 0-15-269958-9

Shaka, King of the Zulus,
Diane Stanley & Peter Vennema
Story of the young Zulu outcast who, through brilliance and determination, rose to become a mighty warrior and leader of his people.
Ages 6-10, Grade levels 1-5
ISBN: 0-688-07343-3

A Story, a Story, Haley, Gail
An African tale--this is the story about how all stories began. Nyame, the sky God sold his stories to Ananse, the Spider Man, so all the children in the world would have stories to listen to.
ISBN: 0689712014

Village Of Round and Square Houses,
Ann Grifalconi
A grandmother explains to her listeners why in their village on the side of a volcano the men live in square houses and the women in round ones.
Ages 5-8, Grade levels K-3
ISBN: 0-316-32862-6

Why Mosquitoes Buzz in Peoples,
Aardema, Verdema
Winner of the Caldecott Medal, this is a beautiful illustrated African folktale.
Ages 4-7, Grade levels K-2
ISBN: 0-8037-6087-6; 0-8037-6088-4

Wildlife Conservation and Tourism in Kenya,
Nyeki, Daniel M.
Offers young adult readers an in-depth study of wildlife conservation in Kenya today.
Ages 12-up, Grade levels 7-up,
ISBN: 9966-884-96-3

Zomo the Rabbit, McDermott, Gerald
A Trickster tale from West Africa, Zomo the rabbit, an African trickster, sets out to gain wisdom.
Grade level PreK-2
ISBN: 0-15-299967-1

A Long Hard Journey, McKissack, Patricia
The story of the Pullman Porters.
Grade levels 6-7
ISBN: 0-8027-6885-7

A Million Fish...More or Less, McKissack, Patricia
Grade levels 4-8
ISBN: 0679906924

A Promise to the Sun, Mollel, T

A Wave in Her Pocket, Joseph, Lynn
ISBN: 0395544327

Abby, Caines, Jeannette
An adopted sister is just as pesky as any other sister and just as lovable.
Grade levels K-2
ISBN: 0064430499

Adventures of High John, the Conqueror,
Sanfield, Steve
Tales of an enslaved African who could outwit the master any time!
All grades
ISBN: 0531084078

The Adventures of Spider, Arkhurst, Joyce
Six Anansi stories retold for younger children.
ISBN: 5-0316-05107-1

African American Achievers Series (vol. I, II, III)
Biographies of African Americans who have achieved great things in the field of science.

African Dreams, Greenfield, Eloise
A black child's dreams are filled with the images of the people and places in Africa.
Grade levels 2-3
ISBN: 0-690-04776-2

Afro-bets Book of Black Heroes from A-Z,
Hudson, W. & Wesley, V.
Ages 3-8, Grade levels Pre K-3
ISBN: 0-940975-02-5

Aida, Price, Leontyne
Opera star Leontyne Price tells the story of an Ethiopian princess with the help of beautiful illustration by award-winners Leo and Diane Dillon.
All ages, All grades,
ISBN: 015200405X

Ajeemah and His Son, Berry, J.
ISBN: 0060210443

Alice, Goldberg, Whoopi
While there are similarities to the traditional **Alice in Wonderland** story, this is definitely a 1990s story with Whoopi Goldberg's Alice braving the peculiarities of New York.

The All Jahdu Story Book, Hamilton, V. Zeely
Grade levels 6-7
ISBN: 0152394982

All Night, All Day, Bryan Ashley
A child's collection of African-American spirituals.
Grade levels 4-5
ISBN: 0689316623

Alvin Ailey, Pinkney, A. D.
Grade levels 4-5
ISBN: 1562824147

Amazing Grace, Hoffman, Mary
Charming story of a little girl determined to play Peter Pan in a school production although she is black and a girl. Ages 4-8, Grade levels K-3
ISBN: 0-8037-1040-2

Amifika, Clifton, Lucille
In making room for Amifika's dad who is returning home from military service, his mother seeks to get rid of things he won't remember.
Ages 6-7, Grade levels 1-2
ISBN: 0-525-25548-6

Amos Fortune: Free Man, Yates, Elizabeth
An 18th century African prince is captured, enslaved and brought to Massachusetts where he works until he can buy his freedom at 60 years old.
Grade levels 5-6
ISBN: 0-525-25570-2; 0-14-034158-7

An Island Christmas, Joseph, Lynn
ISBN: 0-395587611

Anansi & the Moss Covered Rock, Kimmel, Eric
The infamous spider of African and Caribbean folktales discovers a way to trick his neighbors our of their goods. See how the tables are turned!
Ages 5-9, Grade levels k-4
ISBN: 0-8234-0689-X

Anansi Finds a Fool,
Lazy Anansi seeks to trick someone into doing the heavy work of laying his fish trap, but instead he is fooled into doing the job himself.
Grade levels K-3
ISBN: 0803711654

Anansi the Spider, McDermott, Gerald
Another look at the dealings of the trickster of African folklore.
Ages 5-9, Grade levels K-4,
ISBN: 0805003118

Anansi the Spider Man, Sherlock, Sir Philip
Jamaican folk tales about Br'er Anansi, sometimes a man and sometimes a spider.
Grade levels K-3

Ashanti to Zulu, Mustgrove, Margaret
Explains traditions and customs of twenty-six African ethnic groups
beginning with the letters of the alphabet.
Grade levels K-3
ISBN: 0-8037-0358-9

Anthony Burns: The Defeat and Triumph of a Fugitive Slave, Hamilton, Virginia
Through the telling of a story of the trial of a runaway enslaved African, Virginia Hamilton gives a vivid portrayal of the Holocaust of African Enslavement.
Ages 12-16, Grade levels 7-9
ISBN: 0-394-98185-5

Arilla Sun Down, Hamilton, Virginia
The defeat and triumph of a fugitive enslaved African.
Ages 10-11, Grades levels 5-6

At the Crossroads, Isadora, R.
Ages 3-8, Grade levels Pre-K-3
ISBN: 0688052711

Aunt Flossie's Hats (and Crab Cakes Later), Howard, Elizabeth
Two little girls find a world of delight in visiting their Aunt Flossie who has a story for each of her many hats.
Ages 4-7, Grade levels Pre K-2,
ISBN: 0-395-54682-6

Aunt Harriet's Underground Railroad in the Sky, Ringgold, Faith
A tale of the legendary Underground Railroad as experienced by Casie and her brother as they follow Harriet Tubman and learn to understand the meaning of freedom.
Ages 8-12, Grade levels 3-7
ISBN: 0517587688

A Wave in Her Pocket, Joseph, Lynn
Stories from Trinidad
Ages 8-12
ISBN: 0395544327

Baby Animals, Wise-Brown, Margaret
Nicely drawn book on one day in the life of the people
and animals on a farm. Awakes all to the beauty of
nature.
Ages 3-5, Grade levels K-1
ISBN: 0394920406

Baby Says, Steptoe, John
Story of a little boy and his baby brother. This picture
book is carried by images which are universal.
Ages 3-5, Grade levels K-1
ISBN: 0688074235

Back Home, Pinkney, Gloria J.
Eight-year-old Ernestine returns to visit relatives on the
North Carolina farm where she was born.
Ages 6-9, Grade levels 1-4
ISBN: 0-88037-1169-7

Ballad of Belle Dorcas,
Belle Dorcas is a free black woman who chooses to
marry an enslaved African. She thinks of a
unique plan to free him that uses the skill of a "conjure
woman."
Ages 7-13, Grade levels 2-8
ISBN: 0394946456

The Banza, Wolkstein, Diane
Story of the friendship between a tiger and a "banza"-
playing goat.
ISBN: 0-8037-0428-3

Bells of Christmas, Hamilton, Virginia
Virginia Hamilton's story of a middle class black
family's celebration of Christmas in 1890 and one
child's curiosity about how Christmas will be
celebrated in the years to come.
Grade levels 4-7
ISBN: 0-15-206450-8

Benjamin Banneker, Patterson, Lillie
This is a young reader's biography of the black
scientist who demonstrated mathematical abilities
and inventive genius.
Grade levels 1-5
ISBN: 0-687-02900-7

Benjie, Lexau, Joan M.
Ages 6-7, Grade levels 1-2

Benjie on His Own, Lexau, Joan M.
How Benjie conquers the seeming insensitivity of his
neighborhood when his grandmother
becomes sick. A realistic picture book.
Ages 8-9, Grade levels 3-4

Ben's Trumpet, Isadore, Rachel
With striking black and white illustrations, this book
tells the story of Ben who wants to be a trumpeter
but only has an imaginary instrument.
Ages 4-7, Grade levels K-2
ISBN: 0-688-80194-3

The Best Bug to Be, Johnson, Dolores
Kelly is disappointed at getting the role of a
bumblebee instead of a lead role in the school play.
But she soon makes her part the best one of all.
Grade levels Pre-K-4
ISBN: 0027478424

Big Friend, Little Friend, Green, Carol
A little boy looks at the fun he has with his two
friends, one who is bigger than he and one who is
smaller.
Age 3, Grade level Pre - K
ISBN: 0-86316-204-5

Bigmama's, Crews, Donald
See why taking the train to "Bigmama's" farm during
the summer was the highlight of one boy's
childhood.
Ages 4-9, Grade levels Pre-K-4,
ISBN: 0-688-09951-3

Bimwili & the Zimwi, Aardema, Verna
A young girl is abducted by a Zimwi and told to be the
voice inside his drum.
Ages 4-8, Grade levels k-3
ISBN: 0-8037-0213-2

Birthday, Steptoe, John
Grade levels Pre-K-3

The Black B. C's, Clifton, Lucille
The alphabet provides a unifying theme for prose and poetry by describing the achievements of black men and women in history.
ISBN: 0690046596

Black Dance In America, Haskins, J.
Grade levels 7-8
ISBN: 0690046596

Black Heroes of the Wild West, Pelz, Ruth
Stories of eight black Americans who changed the West.
Ages 8-12, Grade levels 3-7
ISBN: 0-940880-25-3

Black Is Brown Is Tan, Adoff, Arnold
Describes in verse the life of brown-skinned Mamma, white-skinned Daddy, their children, and assorted relatives.
Age 5, Grade level Kindergarten
ISBN: 0-06-020084-7

The Black Snowman, Mendez, Phil
An African storyteller's magic *kente* brings to life a snowman who helps Jacob feel good about himself and his black heritage.
Ages 6-12, Grade levels 1-7
ISBN: 0-5990-44873-0

Black Heroes of the American Revolution, Davis, Burk
An account of the black soldiers, sailors, spies, scouts, guides, and wagoners who participated and sacrificed in the struggle for U.S. independence.
Ages 8-12, Grade levels 3-7
ISBN: 0-15-208561-0

Black History for Beginners, Dennis, Denise
Ages 7-10, Grade levels 2-5
ISBN: 0-86316-06897

The Black Mother Goose, Oliver, Elizabeth Murphy
Traditional nursery rhymes with black illustrations.
Ages Infant-6

Black Theatre in America, Haskins, J.
Grade levels 8-9
ISBN: 0-690-04-129-2

Blue Tights, Williams-Garcia, Rita
A high school girl finds confidence and fulfillment after she discovers African dance.
Ages 8-12, Grade levels 3-7
ISBN: 0-533-28293-X

Book of Black Heroes, A-Z,
Biographies of African Americans who have contributed to the American society.
ISBN: 0-940975-27-0

Booker T. Washington, Patterson, Lillie

Boss Cat, Hunter, Kristin
An amusing story of an urban family who acquires a black cat despite the mother's superstitious fears.
Ages 8-9, Grade levels 3-4
ISBN: 0-684-12491-2

Boy & the Ghost,
In a story with roots in African American folklore, a giant rewards a poor boy with a treasure when the boy proves he is both brave and generous.

Boy Who Didn't Believe in Spring, Clifton, Lucille
Two young boys start on an intense investigation of their neighborhood to discover if Spring really exists.
Ages 7-9, Grade levels 2-4
ISBN: 0-525-27145-7

Breadsticks and Blessing Places, Boyd, C.
ISBN: 0-02-709290-9

Brer Rabbit and The Wonderful Tar Baby, Glover, D.

The Bridges of Summer, Seabrooke, Brenda
Zarah didn't want to go and visit somebody she did not know, even if it was her grandmother!
What would she do on this small island off the coast of South Carolina? She wanted to dance, and she would miss her ballet classes! By the end of summer Zarah is transformed because of this visit, learning about her culture and family's past...she was really Princess Zarah!
Grade levels 6-7
ISBN: 0525650946

Bright Eyes, Brown Skin, Hudson, Cheryl
Spend one day in pre-school with four lovely children.
Grade levels 1-2
ISBN: 0-940975-10-6; 0-940975-23-8

Bringing the Rain to Kapiti Plain, Aardema, Verna
A rhythmic read-aloud tale tells how Ki-pat ingeniously brings rain to the arid Kapiti Plain.
Ages 4-6, Grade levels K-1,
ISBN: 0803709048

Brown Angels, Myers, Walter Dean
Poetry and historic photographs of children.
Grade levels 4-5
ISBN: 006022187

Brown Honey in Broomwheat Tea, Thomas, J.
Poetry with illustrations.
Ages 6-up, Grade levels 3-up
ISBN: 0060210885

Brown is a Beautiful Color, Bond, Jean Carey
Ages 6-7, Grade levels 1-2

Brother to the Wind, Walter, Mildred Pitts
With the help of good snake, an African boy gets his fondest wish.
Ages 3-6, Grade levels Pre-K-1
ISBN: 0-688-03812-3

Buffalo Soldiers,
True account of the African American who served in the U.S. Cavalry in the Old West.
Ages 9-12, Grade levels 4-7
ISBN: 0-679-74203-4

Calypso Alphabet, Agard, John
Presents the twenty-six letters of the alphabet using Caribbean words with definitions.
Ages 5-10, Grade levels K-5
ISBN: 0805011773

Can't Sit Still, Lotz, K.
Ages 3-8, Grade levels K-3
ISBN: 0-525-45066-1

Caribbean Alphabet, Lessac, Frane
ISBN: 0-688-12953-6

Caribbean Canvas, Lessac, Frane
Grade levels 5-6
ISBN: 0397323689

Caribbean Carnival, Lessac, Frane
Traditional songs from the island are featured in easy piano and guitar arrangement by the author of **Caribbean Canvas**. Expand horizon in this delightful sing-along book!
Ages 5-9, Grade levels K-4
ISBN: 0397323689

Carousel, Cruz, Donald
ISBN: 0-688-00909-3

Carry, Go, Bring, Come, Samuels, Vyanne
As the household gets ready for a wedding, a little boy finds that he must carry, go, bring, and come until it all gets to be a little too much. Cute!
Ages 4-6, Grade levels K-1
ISBN: 0-688-10780-X

Cat in the Mirror, Stolz, Mary
Ages 10-11, Grades 5-6
ISBN: 0060258330

Charlie Parker Played Be Bop, Roshchka, C.
Delightful look at the legendary musician.
Grade levels 1-2
ISBN: 0531085996

Charlie Pippin, Boyd, C.
For a class project, Charlie elects to study the
Vietnam War, which her father always refuses to
discuss with her. Along the way, she learns that
individuals, including children, can make a difference.
Grade levels 5-8
ISBN: 0027263509

Cherries, and Cherry Pits, Williams, Vera B.
Bidemmi, a young girl who loves to draw, tells four
unconnected stories unified by the theme of cherries
and cherry pits.
Ages 4-8, Grade levels K-3
ISBN: 0688051464

Childtimes, Greenfield, Eloise
A three-generation memoir.
ISBN: 0690038755

Children of Fire,
Eleven-year-old Hallelujah, an orphaned daughter of a
runaway enslaved African, discovers a world that
can be harsh and bigoted, but also exciting and
challenging during the Great Chicago Fire of 1871.
Ages 8-12, Grade levels 3-7
ISBN: 0689316550

Children of Long Ago, Little, Lessie Jones
Poems reflecting simpler days, with grandmothers
who read aloud and children who walk barefoot and
pick blackberries.
Grade levels 4-5
ISBN: 0399214739

Children of Promise, Sullivan, C.
An anthology of art and literature by African
Americans for children.
Grade levels 6-12
ISBN: 0810931702

Chilly Stomach, Craines, Jeanette
ISBN: 0060209763

Chita's Christmas Tree, Howard, Elizabeth
Near the turn of the century, the celebration of
Christmas means wonderful times for a little girl
named Chita, but none more wonderful than going
with father to find her own special Christmas
tree.
Ages 5-8, Grade levels K-3
ISBN: 0-02-74621-2

Christmas Feasts and Festivals, Patterson, Lillie
Topics such as Christmas music, national legendary
gift givers (Santa Claus, Father Christmas, etc.),
the holiday feast, and use of greens enjoy separate
chapters.

Circle of Gold, Boyd, C.
Grade levels 5-6

Clean Your Room Harvey Moon, Cummings, Pat
Harvey wants to watch TV. His mom wants his
room cleaned.
ISBN: 0-689-71798-9

Climbing Jacob's Ladder, Langstaff, John
Heroes of the Bible in African-American Spirituals
Grade levels 4-5
ISBN: 0689504942

Coconut Kind of Day, Joseph, Lynn
A collection of poems depicting the sight and sounds
of the Caribbean islands.
Ages 5-8, Grade levels K-8
ISBN: 0688091202

Cornrows, Yarbrough, Camille
Explains how the cornrows hairstyle, a symbol of
Africa since ancient times, can symbolize the
courage of outstanding African Americans today.
Ages 6-9, Grade levels 1-4,
ISBN: 0-698-20529-4

Cousins, Hamilton, Virginia
One of Virginia Hamilton's most stirring novels,
Cousins tells the story of five remarkable cousins
who are strong and individual.
Grade levels 5-8
ISBN: 0399221646

Cover,
A ten-year-old black girl from a small town in South Carolina chronicles her bewildering but deepening relationship with her white stepmother after the death of her father only hours after the wedding.

Crocodile and Hen, Lexau, Joan M.

Crystal, Myers, Walter Dean
A beautiful 16-year-old model discovers that her glamorous career has a dark side.
Grade levels 7-12
ISBN: 0670804266

Daddy, Caines, Jeannette
A warm and loving story of Windy and her daddy who shared special moments together when he picks her up on Saturdays.
Garde levels K-2
ISBN: 0060209240

Daddy and I, Greenfield, Eloise
A board book in which a young boy tells about the fun he has with his dad.
Ages 2-5, Grade levels Pre-K-K

Daddy Is a Monster Sometimes, Steptoe, J.
Two children describe how their father turns into a scary monster when they have done something wrong.
Ages 5-8, Grade levels K-3
ISBN: 0-397-31893-6

Dancing Granny, Bryan, Ashley
The trickster Ananse gets Granny started dancing so he can raid her garden, but his own trick does him in.
Ages 4-7, Grade levels K-2
ISBN: 0-689-71149-2

Dancing With the Indians Medearis, Angela
Ages 5-7, Grade levels K-2
ISBN: 0-8234-0893-0

Daniel's Dog, Bogart, JoEllen
A little boy feels left out when a new baby comes into the house. He makes up an imaginary dog as his companion but soon learns that the new baby did not leave him out of his mom's affection.
Ages 4-7, Grade levels K-2
ISBN: 0590434020

Dark-Thirty: Southern Tales of the Supernatural, McKissack, Patricia
A collection of ghost stories with African American themes, designed to be told during the dark thirty—the half hour before sunset—when ghosts seem all too believable.
Ages 8-12, Grade levels 3-7
ISBN: 0679918639

The Dark Way, Hamilton, Virginia
ISBN: 0152223401

Darkness And The Butterfly, Grifalconi, Ann
Small Osa is fearless during the day, climbing trees or exploring the African valley where she lives, but at night she becomes afraid of the strange and terrifying things that might lie in the dark.
Ages 4-7, Grade levels K-2
ISBN: 0316328634

Day of the Rainbow,
On a hot summer day in South Africa, three cranky people each lose something precious to them. A rainbow helps each to find their treasure.
Ages 5-7, Grade levels K-2
ISBN: 0-670-82456-9

(The) Day They Stole the Letter "J"

Daydreamers, Eloise Greenfield
Rhymes that highlight the daydreams of African American children.
Ages 4-7, Grade levels K-2
ISBN: 0803701675

The Dear One, Woodson, J.
Grade Levels 5-6
ISBN: 0385304161

Definitely Cool, Wilkinson, Brenda
Grade Levels 5-6
ISBN: 0590461869

Designed by God, So I Must Be Special,
Sose, Bonnie
Colorful book for ages 3-7 that discusses the gifts that God has given to all his creations, and the gift each is to the other.
Ages 3-7, Grade levels Pre-K-2
ISBN: 0-9615279-4-3

Diana Ross, Haskins, James
Biography of the former Supreme and singing star/performer.
Ages 7-11, Grade levels 2-7

Dinner At Aunt Connie's House, Ringgold, F.
Grade levels Pre-K-6
ISBN: 1562824260

The Disappearance, Guy, R.

Do Like Kyla, Angela Johnson
Story of a young girl's love for and desire to imitate an older sister.
Ages 8-9, Grade levels 3-4
ISBN: 0-531-08452-3

Doctor Shawn, Breinburg, Petronella
Mom goes shopping and leaves the children alone with instructions not to mess the house. They play doctor with Shawn as the doctor and his sister as the nurse.
Ages 4-5, Grade levels Pre-K-K
ISBN: 0690007221

Don't You Remember, Clifton, Lucille
Four-year-old Tate remembers special promises from her parents, and she also wants to drink coffee with her older brothers. But they all forget until, on her birthday, special requests are remembered.
Ages 8-9, Grade levels 3-4
ISBN: 0-525-28840-6

Down in Piney Woods, Smothers, Ethel
Grade levels 5-7
ISBN: 0679903607

The Drinking Gourd, Monjo, F. M.
Sent home alone for misbehaving in church, Tommy discovers that his house is a station on the Underground Railroad.
Ages 6-7, Grade levels 1-2,
ISBN: 0064440427

Drylongso, Hamilton, Virginia
As a great wall of dust moves across their drought-stricken farm, a black family's distress is relieved by a young man called Drylongso, who literally blows into their lives with the storm.
Ages 8-11, Grade levels 3-6
ISBN: 0152242414

Duke Ellington, Collier, Ames
Grade levels 5-6
ISBN: 0027229858

Dustland, Hamilton, Virginia
This sequel to *Justice and Her Brothers* shows eleven-year-old Justice discovering that she has supersensory powers as do her friend and her twin brothers.
ISBN: 0-15-224315-1

Ears and Tails and Common Sense,
Sherlock, Sir Philip
More stories from the Caribbean.
ISBN: 0-690-00450-8

Efan the Great, Schotter, Roni
A young boy finds a way to give his family the Christmas tree they can't afford.
Ages 9-11, Grade levels 4-6
ISBN: 0 -688-04987-7

The Egypt Game, Myers, Walter Dean
Two girls, one Black and one white, decide to play the Egypt Game and develop a group of loyal players until something begins to happen to the players.
Ages 12-up, Grade levels 6-12
ISBN: 0689300069

18 Pine St. Myers, Walter Dean
A series of five books which follow the adventures of
students at Murphy High School and their
favorite hangout, the pizza parlor at 18 Pine St.
Ages 10-up, Grade levels 5-up

Elephant's Wrestling Match, Sierra, Judy
All the animals of the forest challenge the mighty
elephant to a wrestling match, but it takes brains,
not might to defeat him.
ISBN: 0525673660

Elijah's Angel, Rosen, Michael J.
A story for Chanukah and Christmas.
A young Jewish boy and an old black barber are
friends and exchange gifts, showing that
friendship cuts across the boundaries of religious
differences.
Grade levels K-5
ISBN: 0-15-225394-7

Emily and the Klunky Baby and the Next-Door Dog,
Lexau, Joan M
ISBN: 0-8037-2309-1

Enchanted Hair Tale, DeVeaux, A.
Met with a negative reaction to his dreadlocks by
teachers and school friends, Sudan discovers a way to
belong while still remaining true to himself.
Ages 5-8, Grade levels K-3
ISBN: 0-06-443271-8

Escape From Slavery, Rappaport, Doreen
Exciting and inspiring stories of five enslaved African
Americans who managed to find freedom before the
Civil War.
Age 12, Grade level 7
ISBN: 0060216328

Escape to Freedom, Davis, Ossie
A play about young Frederick Douglass.
Born a slave, young Frederick Douglass endures many
years of cruelty before escaping to the North to claim
his freedom.
Grade levels 4-5
ISBN: 0-14-03435505

Evans Corner, Starr Hill, Elizabeth
Evan longs for a place that is all his own in his
family's crowded apartment.
Ages 3-8, Grade levels Pre-K-3
ISBN: 0670828300

Everett Anderson's Christmas Coming,
Clifton, Lucille
Experience Everett's joy as his favorite holiday
approaches.
Ages 4-8, Grade levels Pre K-3
ISBN: 0805015493

Everett Anderson's Goodbye, Clifton, Lucille
Everett has a difficult time dealing with his father's
death.
Ages 4-8, Grade levels Pre K-3
ISBN: 0805008004

Everett Anderson's Nine Months Long,
Clifton, Lucille
Everett's mom has remarried and is expecting another
child and he must deal with his feelings of his mom
being different and his place in the new family.
Ages 4-8, Grade levels Pre-K-3
ISBN: 0805002952

Everett Anderson's Year, Clifton, Lucille
Everett's seventh year of life is described in twelve
poems which reveal the intimacy of his
immediate world.
Grade levels K-4
ISBN: 0805022473

Every Man Heart Lay Down, Graham, Lorenz
This African retelling and interpretation of events of
the first Christmas comes from the author's
collection of retold Bible stories - How God Fix Jonah
ISBN: 563971844

Extraordinary Black Americans, Altman, Susan
Short biographies of 95 black Americans from Colonial
to contemporary times, highlighting their
personal achievements and their resulting
contributions to the growth of American society.
Grade levels 4-12
ISBN: 0516005812

Fallen Angels, Myers, Walter Dean
A gripping and authentic depiction of the brutality of war as seen through the eyes of a black teenager on a tour of duty in Vietnam.
Ages 13-up, Grade levels 8-up
ISBN: 0590409425

Famous American Negroes, Hughes, Cheryl
Biographies of well-known and less well-known black Americans are presented to young readers.

Famous Negro Athletes, Bontemps, Arna
Biographies present the struggle of each subject to succeed as both athlete and person. Included are Joe Louis, Sugar Ray Robinson, Jackie Robinson, Leroy (Satchel) Paige, Willie Mays, Jesse Owens, Willie Brown, and Althea Gibson.

Famous Negro Music Makers, Hughes, Cheryl
These are short biographical sketches of African Americans who have achieved fame or made a large contribution to music. Groups such as the Fisk Jubilee Singers are included.

Fannie Lou Hamer, Jordan, June
A black woman with only a sixth-grade education assumed leadership for registering blacks to vote. Of many highlights of Hamer's life, she was jailed and beaten, founded the Freedom Farm Cooperative, and became a public figure.
Grade level 4-5
ISBN: 0-690-28893-X

Fashion by Tasha, Johnson, S.

Fast Sam, Cool Clyde, and Stuff,
Myers, Walter Dean
An unusual group of boys and girls who together grow to know the meaning of friendship. Funny and warm.
Ages 11-14, Grade levels 6-9
ISBN: 0670308749

Father and Son, Lautere, D.
A father and son decide to spend a sunny afternoon together flying their kite and having fun.
Ages 3-6, Grade levels Pre-K-1
ISBN: 039921867-X

Femi and Old Grandaddie, Robinson, Adjai
ISBN: 0-698-30453-5

Ferris Wheel, Stolz, Mary
Ages 10-11, Grade levels 5-6
ISBN: 0060258608

Finding the Green Stone,
Symbolic and sensitive tale of a little boy who loses his green (happiness and fulfillment) and discovers that those things really come from within.
Ages 7-12, Grade levels 2-7
ISBN: 0-15-227538-X

First Pink Light, Greenfield, Eloise
A little boy's father has been away on a long trip, but he is returning home at dawn the next day.
The son tries to stay up until the "first pink light" when Dad will surely appear.
Ages 5-8, Grade levels K-3
ISBN: 0-86316-212-6

Flossie and the Fox, McKissack, Patricia
Flossie is sent on an errand by her mother and told to watch out for the Fox. But Flossie outfoxes the Fox.
Ages 5-8, Grade levels K-3
ISBN: 0803702515

Fly, Jimmy, Fly, Myers, Walter Dean
Jimmy's inner city world is explored through a quiet, suggestive, fluent prose poem as he dreams of flying like a bird.
Grade levels K-3
ISBN: 0399608842

Follow the Drinking Gourd, Winter, Jeanette
A "conductor" on the Underground Railroad leads a band of slaves to freedom by following the stars known as the drinking gourd.
Ages 5-7, Grade levels K-2,
ISBN: 0-394-99694-1

For the Life of Laetitia, Hodge, M.
ISBN: 0374324476

Forever Friends, Boyd, C.
Grade levels 5-6
ISBN: 0-14-032077-6

Frederick Douglass, Bontemps, Arna
This book chiefly covers the boyhood and youth of the first great black abolitionist--the early years that were dramatized by the awakening of a human spirit trapped by an inhumane system, the escape from the holocaust of African enslavement, and the beginning of a career dedicated to the cause of freedom for all men.

Freedom's Children, Levine, Ellen
Young civil rights activists tell their own stories. A collection of oral histories of 30 African Americans who were teenagers in the 1950s and 1960s as they talk about what it was like for them in Alabama, Mississippi and Arkansas: sitting in, riding at the front of the bus, integrating schools, and braving arrest.
Grade levels 7-12
ISBN: 0-399-21893-9

Freedom Songs, Moore, Y.
Grade levels 7-9
ISBN: 0531084124

Freight Train, Crews, Donald
This train book presents colors and the different card of a train that move in and out of a tunnel, past cities, and across trestles on track along the bottom of the page.
Ages 4-5, Grade levels Pre-K-K
ISBN: 0688129404

The Friends, Guy, R.
ISBN: 0553205951

The Friendship, Taylor, Mildred D.
In a Mississippi town in the 1930s, Cassie Logan and her brothers are witness to the unforgettable confrontation between Tom, an old black man, and a white storekeeper he has always called by his first name.
Ages 6-7, Grade levels 1-2,
ISBN: 0-8037-0418-6

Friendship and the Gold Cadillac, Taylor, Mildred
These are extremely well written stories, the type that can take a child off into another place and time.
Ages 8-12 Grade levels 3-7
ISBN: 0553257655

From Miss Ida's Porch, Belton, S
Grade levels 3-7
ISBN: 0027089150.

Front Porch Stories, Tate, E.
A father shares family stories with his daughter and niece about life in their small town.
Ages 7-11, Grade levels 2-6
ISBN: 0553083848

Galimoto, Williams, Karen
A seven-year-old African child walks through his village trying to find the materials to make a special toy.
Ages 5-8, Grade levels K-3,
ISBN: 0688087892

Games to Play, Verstraete, E.
Multicultural images illustrate this book of popular children's rhymes.
ISBN: 1562880519

The Gathering, Hamilton, Virginia
In this last book of the trilogy, the four children with supersensory powers return to Dustland to battle Mal, a powerful force of the future. The other titles are *Justice and Her Brothers* and *Dustland*.
ISBN: 0-688-84269-0

George Washington Carver, Green, Carol
Grade levels K-4
ISBN: 0516042505

Get on Board, Haskins, J.
Grade levels 4-11
ISBN: 0590454188

Gift-Giver, Hensen, Joyce
A sensitive portrayal of a ten-year-old girl's coming of age. Offers a positive perspective on life in the inner city and shows that a "ghetto" is a place where people hope, grow, and care.
Ages 9-12, Grade levels 4-6,
ISBN: 089919852X

Girl Called Boy, Hurmence, Belinda
When a middle-class African American girl is mysteriously transported back into enslavement times, she discovers that most enslaved Africans were courageous people.
Ages 11-14, Grade levels 6-9
ISBN: 0-395-55698-8

The Girl Who Wore Snakes, Johnson, Angela
ISBN: 0531086410

Golden Bear, Young, R.
Grade levels Pre-K-2
ISBN: 0670825778

Good Morning Baby, Hudson, C. & Wesley, V.
Small children are sure to enjoy sharing the familiar rituals of waking up and getting ready for bed depicted through rhyming text and friendly realistic illustration of African American babies.
Ages 6mo-3yrs, Grade level Pre-K
ISBN: 0-590-45760-8

Good Night Baby, Hudson, C. & Wesley, V.
Small children are sure to enjoy sharing the familiar rituals of waking up and getting ready for bed depicted through rhyming text and friendly realistic illustration of African American babies.
Ages 6mo-3yrs, Grade level Pre-K
ISBN: 0-590-45761-6

Go Fish, Stolz, Mary
The grandfather and grandson team from *Storm in the Night* are back with a delightful tale of an eventful fishing trip together.
Ages 7-11, Grade levels 2-6
ISBN: 0060258225

Go Free or Die, Ferris, Jeri
The Story of Harriet Tubman: A dramatic retelling of the life of this conductor on the Underground Railroad. For younger readers
ISBN: 0876143176

Going Swimming, Berridge, Celia / Random House
Grade levels 4-5
ISBN: 0803703430

The Gold Cadillac. Taylor, Mildred D.

Golden Bear, Young, Ruth
Small boy and his stuffed bear tell about the fun they have together. Great book for pre-schoolers.
Ages 1 1/2-4, Grade level Pre K
ISBN: 0670825778

The Golden Lynx, Baker, Augusta
Folktales from seven countries and selections from out-of-print books are included because they have stood the supreme test of children's interest and approval.

The Golden Pasture, Thomas, Joyce Carol
Estranged for many years, a boy and his father are reunited through the love of a horse.
Ages 10-11, Grade levels 5-6
ISBN: 0-590-33681-9

Good News: Formerly Bubbles, Greenfield, Eloise
When a little boy comes home from school excited about his ability to read, he isn't able to capture his busy mother's attention, so he tells his baby sister who is too young to understand.
Ages 8-9, Grade levels 3-4
ISBN: 0-698-30651-1

Grandma's Joy, Greenfield, Eloise
A little girl tries to cheer up her despondent grandmother by reminding her of her love.
Ages 6-9, Grade levels 1-4
ISBN: 0399210644

Grandpa's Face, Greenfield, Eloise
A little girl's love for her actor grandfather is threatened when she is frightened by a face she sees him make during rehearsal.
Ages 5-8, Grade levels K-3,
ISBN: 0399215255

The Great Migration, Lawrence, Jacob
Ages 7-up, Grade levels 2, 3 and 4
ISBN: 0060230371

The Great Rebellion, Stolz, Mary
Ages 8-9, Grade levels 3-4

The Green Lion of Zion Street, Fields, Julia
Ages 8-9, Grade levels 3-7
ISBN: 0689504144

Growing, Grimes, Nikki
Ages 10-11, Grade levels 5-6
ISBN: 0140370668

Half a Moon & One Whole Star,
Dragonwagon, Crescent
A beautiful drawn book of poetry.
Ages 5-8, Grade levels K-3
ISBN: 0-68971415-7

Happy Birthday Martin Luther King, Marzollo, Jean
Grade levels Pre-k-4
ISBN: 0590440659

Harbor, Crews, Donald
ISBN: 0-688-00862-3

Hard to Be Six, Adoff, A.
A six-year-old boy who wants to grow up fast learns a
lesson about patience from his grandfather.
Ages 6-9, Grade levels 2-3
ISBN: 0688095798

Harriet and the Promised Land, Lawrence, J.
Grade levels 2-3
ISBN: 0-671-86673-7

Harriet Tubman, Petry, Ann
Conductor of the Underground Railroad.
The text of this book has the same strength and
dignity as its subject.
Ages 10-11, Grade levels 5-6
ISBN: 1-559-05097-7

Have a Happy Kwanzaa, Walter, Mildred Pitts
Chris wants a bicycle for his birthday, which falls on
Christmas, but his father is temporarily out of work.
As preparations begin for the celebration of Kwanzaa,
Chris realizes how much support and love comes from
his family and friends.
Ages 8-10, Grade levels 3-5
ISBN: 0-688-06924-X

Hear My Cry, Taylor, Mildred
Grade levels 5-6
ISBN: 0803774737

Hi Cat!, Keats, Ezra Jack
On his way to meet Peter, Archie sees someone new
on the block—a cat.
Ages 6-7, Grade levels 1-2,
ISBN: 0-8037-0418-6

Holes and Peeks, Jonas, Ann
A little girl discusses her fear of holes (such as in her
shoes or the drain in the bath tub) and her joy
at peeks (when playing peek-a-boo).
Ages 3-7, Grade levels Pre-K-2
ISBN: 0-688-02538-2

Home Place, DragonWagon, Crescent
A family wandering through the woods finds objects
that make them wonder about the family that
had lived there.
Grade levels Pre-K-3
ISBN: 0027331903

Honey, I Love, Greenfield, Eloise
Sixteen love poems are shown from the point of view
of a child.
Ages 6-9, Grade levels 1-4,
ISBN: 0-690-03845-3

Hoops, Myers, Walter Dean
A 17-year-old basketball player is plagued by doubt
about himself and his coach as the most
important tournament of the season begins.
Ages 14-up, Grade levels 9-up
ISBN: 0440938848

House of Dies Drear, Hamilton, Virginia
Absorbing mystery surrounding a little boy's search for the secrets of a murdered abolitionist house. Excellent book.
Ages 12-up, Grade levels 7-up
ISBN: 0-02-743500-2; 0-02-04352-7

How Many Spots Does a Leopard Have?
Lester, Julius
A magnificent collection of African and Jewish folktales.
Ages 7-12, Grade levels 2-7,
ISBN: 0590419730

How Many Stars in the Sky?
One evening, a father and son seek a good place to count the stars.
Ages 5-8, Grade levels K-3
ISBN: 0-688-10104-6

How the Leopard Got His Spots, Glower, D.

Hundred Penny Box, Mathis, Sharon Bell
Michael loves his 100-year-old Great-great-aunt Dew who has an old box filled with pennies, one for each of her 100 years. He tries to prevent his mother from getting rid of the elderly woman's "old things."
Ages 9-12, Grade levels 4-7,
ISBN: 0-14-032169-1

I Have a Dream, Davidson, M.
The Story of Martin Luther King Jr.

I Love My Family, Hudson, W.
ISBN: 0590457632

I Make Music, Greenfield , Eloise
A broad book, tells the story of a little girl as she plays various instruments.
Ages 2-5, Grade levels Pre-K-K
ISBN: 0-86316-205-3

I Am a Jesse White Tumbler, Schmidt, D.
Ages 3-8, Grade levels Pre-K-3
ISBN: 0807534447

I Am An Explorer, Moses, Amy
During a trip to the park, a child explores an imaginary cave, mountain, jungle, and desert. From the Rookie Reader series.
Ages 6-8, Grade levels 1-3
ISBN: 0516020595

Imani's Gift at Kwanzaa, Palmon, Denise Burden
A young African American girl learns the meaning and ideas of Kwanzaa and joins her family to celebrate the special holiday for African Americans.
Ages 6-7, Grade levels 1-2
ISBN: 0-671-79841-3

I Need a Lunch Box, Caines, Jeannette
A little boy can't wait to get his first lunch box like his sister who is beginning school.
Ages 5-7, Grade levels K-2
ISBN: 0060209844

I Remember "121", Haskins, Francine
Celebrates the joys of growing up in a traditional African-American family household.
Ages 4-12, Grade levels K-7
ISBN: 0-89239-100-6

Sing to the Sun, Bryan, Ashley
Ages 3-8, Grade levels 2-6
ISBN: 006020833

If You Travelled on the Underground Railroad, Levine, Ellen
ISBN: 059040556X

Iggie's House, Blume, Judy
A white girl gets to know a black family that has moved into her best friend's house, the first black family on her block.
Grade levels 4-5
ISBN: 0440440629

Iguana's Tail, Sherlock, Sir Philip
Crick Crack stories from the Caribbean.
Six short, self-explanatory animal tales are connected by the device of travelers swapping stories to shorten the journey. Each story is introduced and concluded by a traditionally Caribbean, ritualistic, attention-calling dialogue between the story-teller and the audience.

In for Winter,Out for Spring, Adoff, A.
A beautiful book of poetry celebrating the changing of the seasons.
Grade levels K-4
ISBN: 0152386378

In My Aunt Otilla's Spirits, Garcia, Richard
Aunt Otilla comes to visit from Puerto Rico and brings with her "spirits" that change the house!

In the Beginning, Hamilton, Virginia
Twenty-five stories from around the world on the beginning of the earth, humankind and the universe.
All ages, All grades
ISBN: 0152387404

The Inca, McKissack, Patricia
The daily life, religion, government, and present-day descendants of the Incas are presented here.
ISBN: 0516012681

Indigo and the Moonlight Gold, Gilchrist, J.
Grade levels 4 - 5
ISBN: 086316210X

Irene and the Big Fine Nickel, Irene Smalls-Hector
Tells the story of the adventures of a young girl living in Harlem in the 1950s on the morning that she finds a nickel in the street.
Ages 5-8, Grade levels K-3
ISBN: 0316798711

Island Baby, Keller,
Pops, a man who runs a bird hospital on an island, and his young helper, Simon, nurse an injured baby bird back to health.
Ages 3-6, Grade levels Pre-K-1
ISBN: 0688105807

It Ain't All For Nothing, Myers, Walter Dean
ISBN: 0-670-40301-6

Jahdu, Hamilton, Virginia
Carved and lucid beads on a storyteller's chain are linked to form a story about Jahdu who is taunted by other creatures, is told that he has lost his power, and is upset that he has lost his shadow.
Ages 8-9, Grade levels 3-4
ISBN: 0-688-84246-1

Jake and Honeybunch Go to Heaven,
The adventures in heaven of Jake and his only friend, his mule Honeybunch.
Ages 5-8, Grade levels K-3
ISBN: 0-374-33652-0

Jamaica and Brianna, Havill, Juanita
Grade Levels Pre-K-3
ISBN: 0395644895

Jamaica Tag Along, Havill, Juanita
Jamaica's feelings are hurt when her older brother doesn't want her tagging along while he's with his friends. When she gets an unwanted companion, she realizes how she has been treating him as badly as her brother has treated her.
Ages 5-7, Grade levels K-2
ISBN: 0395496020

Jamaica Find, Havill, Juanita
Jamaica finds a stuffed dog she would like to keep. She comes to understand that the owner must love the lost dog as much as she.
Ages 5-7, Grade levels K-2
ISBN: 039545357

Jamal & the Angel, Rodriguez, Anita
Again, we research for you! This is the only book which features a beautiful black angel! Told from the point of view of a young eight-year-old African American male, you will love the colors and his faith! A unique book.
ISBN: 0517586010

Jamal's Busy Day, Hudson, W.
Ages 3 - 8, Grade levels Pre K - 3
ISBN: 0-940975-21-1

Jambo Means Hello, Feelings, M
Grade levels K-3
ISBN: 0803743467

The PictureTtakin' Man.
James Van Der Zee, Haskins, James
Grade levels 7-8
ISBN: 0-86543-261-9

James Weldon Johnson, Egypt, Ophelia
This book is a mildly fictionalized introduction to
Johnson's life, interests, and accomplishments.
ISBN: 0690002157

Lift Every Voice and Sing.
James Weldon Johnson, McKissack, Patricia
ISBN: 0516041746

James Weldon Johnson, Tolbert-Rouchaleau, Jane
A talented educator, songwriter, poet, novelist,
journalist, Diplomat and civil rights leader. Black
Americans of Achievement Series.
Grade levels 6-7
ISBN: 15546596X

Jenny, Beth Wilson
In a series of brief monologues, Jenny shares her
delight in the things that fill her world, from family
and school to bubble baths, a wedding, chocolate
cakes, and the memory of Martin Luther King.
Ages 5-8, Grade levels K-3
ISBN: 002793120X

Jesse Jackson: **A Biography**, McKissack, Patricia
Grade levels 6-7
ISBN: 0590431811

Jimmy Lee Did It, Cummings, Pat
Artie tells his sister that the messes all over the
house are the work of the elusive Jimmie Lee.
Ages 3-6, Grade levels Pre-K-1,
ISBN: 0688046339

John Brown, **A Cry for Freedom**, Graham, Lorenz
ISBN: 0-690-04024-5

John Brown's Raid, Graham, Lorenz
A picture history of the attack on Harper's Ferry,
Virginia.

Jonathan and His Mommy, Small-Hector, I
ISBN: 0-316-79870-3

Josephine's Imagination, Dobrin, Arnold
Josephine uses her imagination and creativity to
help her mom sell brooms.
Ages 4-7, Grade levels K-2,
ISBN: 0590434942

Joshua's Masai Mask, Hru, D.
Grade levels 4-5
ISBN: 1-88000-002-4

Journey, Thomas, J.
ISBN: 0-590-4-0627-2

Julian, Dream Doctor, Cameron, Ann
Julian and Huey try to find the perfect gift for Dad
with amusing results.
Ages 7-9, Grade levels 2-4
ISBN: 0679905243

Julian's Glorious Summer, Cameron, Ann
When his best friend, Gloria, receives a new bike,
seven year old Julian avoids her because he is afraid
of bikes.
Ages 7-9, Grade levels 2-4
ISBN: 0394991176

Julian, **Secret Agent**, Cameron, Ann
A continuation of the Julian tales, Julian and friends
decide to become secret agents and get
themselves into one adventure after another.
Ages 7-9, Grade levels 2-4
ISBN: 0394919491

Juma and the Magic Jinn, Anderson, J.
Bored with school and searching for an adventure,
Juma uncorks the forbidden jinn jar and gets his
three wishes in a manner he had not expected.
ISBN: 0688054439

Jump at De Sun, Porter, A. P.
ISBN: 0876146671

Jump Ship to Freedom, Collier, James
In 1797 a 14-year-old enslaved African, anxious to buy freedom for himself and his mother, escapes from his dishonest master and tries to find help in cashing the soldier's notes received by his father for fighting in the Revolution.
Ages 10-11, Grade levels 5-6
ISBN: 0-440-44323-7

Junius Over Far, Hamilton, Virginia
Grade levels 6-7
ISBN: 006022195X

Just Like Martin, Ossie Davis
Following the death of two classmates in the bombing of an Alabama church, a 14-year-old boy organizes a Civil Rights march in 1963.
Ages 11-15, Grade levels 6-10
ISBN: 0671732021

Just My Luck, Moore, E.
A lonely girl and her new found friend become neighborhood detectives in order to earn money for a pet.
Ages 8-10, Grade levels 3-5
ISBN: 0-14-034790-9

Just Us Women, Caines, Jeannette
A little girl and her favorite aunt take their yearly car trip with only the two of them; no men allowed.
Ages 4-8, Grade levels K-3,
ISBN: 0064430561

Justice and Her Brothers, Hamilton, Virginia
Eleven-year-old Justice spends the summer trying to keep up with her thirteen-year-old twin brothers who take her with them when they travel into the future.
ISBN: 0-15-241640-4

Justin & the Best Biscuits in the World, Walter, Mildred Pitts
Tired of being corrected or scolded by his mother and sisters, and tired of doing housework he sees as "women's work," ten-year-old Justin is delighted to visit his grandfather's ranch. He learns of the proud heritage of the Black cowboy and that "women's work" is done by all.
Ages 8-12, Grade levels 3-7
ISBN: 0679803467

Kimako's Story, Jordan, June
The varied adventures of seven-year-old Kimako and her life in the city.
ISBN: 0-395-60338-2

Kinda Blue, Grifalconi, Ann
Sissy is kinda blue but it's not long before Uncle Dan changes all that by pointing out how people are different and each has special needs.
Ages 3-8, Grade levels Pre-K-3
ISBN: 0316328693

Knee-High Man and Other Tales, Lester, Julius
A collection of African American folktales centered around animals. At one time, many of these stories were actually enslaved/enslaver stories, today, however, most read them simply for fun.
Ages 3-7, Grade levels Pre-K-2
ISBN: 0-8037-0234-5; 0-8037-4607-5

Koya Delaney and the Good Girls Blues, Greenfield, Eloise
Young girl learns to deal with her emotions and to confront difficult situations.
Ages 10-14, Grade levels 5-9
ISBN: 0590433008

Kwanzaa, Porter, A. P.
Describes the origins and practices of Kwanzaa, an African American holiday created to remind African Americans of their history and cultural origins.
Grade levels K-6
ISBN: 0-87614-668-X; 0-87614-545-4

Langston Hughes, American Poet, Walker, Alice
A lively biography of the poet is presented by one whom he inspired.
ISBN: 0-690-00219X

Laney's Lost Momma, Hamm, Diane
A little girl loses her mom in a busy department store.
Ages 3-6. Grade levels Pre-K-1
ISBN: 0807543403

Last Summer with Maizon, Woodson, J.
Grade levels 5-6
ISBN: 038530045X

The Leaving Morning, Johnson, Angela
A little boy and his sister prepare with their family to leave their home for a new one. On the leaving morning, he watches the movers, says good-bye to familiar places and people, and leaves his lip marks on the window.
Ages 3-6 Grade levels Pre-K-1
ISBN: 0-531-08592-9

Legend of Tarik, Myers, Walter Dean
Tarik thought that defeating the savage El Muerte would be victory, but discovers there was no sweetness in vengeance. Set in medieval Africa. For older readers.
ISBN: 0-590-44426-3

Let the Circle Be Unbroken, Taylor, Mildred D.
An award-winning book on the effects of prejudice and the value of family through the eyes of one African American family just before the Civil Rights movement of the 1950s and 1960s.
Grade levels 5 6
ISBN: 0553234366

Let's Be Enemies, Udry, Janice May
Grade levels K-3
ISBN: 0-06-026131-5

Let's Hear It for the Queen, Childress, Alice
ISBN: 0-698-306406

Let's Make Music,

Letters from a Slave Girl, Lyions, Mary
A fictionalized version of the life of Harriet Jacobs, told in the form of letters that she might have written during her enslavement in North Carolina and as she prepared for escape to the North in 1842.
Ages 12-up, Grade levels 7-up
ISBN: 0684194465

Life and Times of a Free Black Man, Hamilton, Virginia

Lift Every Voice and Sing, Johnson, James Weldon
Grade levels 3-4
ISBN: 0590469827

Lillie of Watts, Walter, Mildred Pitts
A birthday discovery book.
Grade levels 3-4

The Lion and the Ostrich's Chicks, Bryan, Ashley
Ages 3-8, Grade levels Pre-K-3
ISBN: 068931311X

Lil' Sis and Uncle Willie, Everett, Gwen
Now our kids can learn about famous African American painters at a young age. After the success of Lil' Sis and Uncle Willie, we see a new trend being set with these art history books for our kids.
ISBN: 0847814629

Little Eight John, Wahl, Jan
A mean little boy persists in disobeying his mother until he finds his mischief backfiring on him.
Ages 4-8, Grade levels K-3
ISBN: 0-525-67367-9

Little Lou,
Pencil etchings depict the life of a little boy growing up in the 1920s and 1930s who wants to play the piano and is determined to let nothing stop him.
Ages 7-up, Grade levels 2-up
ISBN: 0-88682-329-3

A Little Love, Hamilton, Virginia
ISBN: 0-399-21046-6

Stories From Black History.
Long Journey Home, Lester, Julius
An historical fiction, this volume contains six stories about enslaved and former enslaved Africans and how they triumphed over their situations.
Ages 12-up, Grade levels 7-up,
ISBN: 059041433X

(The) Lost Zoo, Cullen, Countee
Written by the late Harlem Renaissance writer, Countee Cullen, as told to him by his precocious pet Christopher Cat, this book of poetry features such wonderful creatures as the Lop-Sided Lizard, the Ha-Ha-Ha, the One-Sided, etc.
Ages 8-10, Grade levels 3-5
ISBN: 0-382-24255-6

Ludell, Wilkinson, Brenda
When Ludell moves from Georgia to New York she has to adjust to big-city living and separation from her boyfriend, Willie.
Ages 10-11, Grade levels 5-6
ISBN: 0-06-026492-6

Ludell and Willie, Wilkinson, Brenda
Grade levels 10-12
ISBN: 0-06-026488-8

Lucky Stone, Clifton, Lucille
Four short stories about four generations of black women and their dealings with a "lucky stone," spanning from the period just before the Emancipation Proclamation to the present.
Ages 8-12, Grade levels 3-7,
ISBN: 0440451108

Mac & Marie & the Train Toss Surprise,
Howard, Elizabeth
Grade levels 2-3
ISBN: 0027446409

Magical Adventure of Pretty Pearl,
Hamilton, Virginia
An African child with special powers travels to the New World on a slave ship and begins a life that will change her forever.
Ages 12-up, Grade levels 7-up
ISBN: 0064401782

Maizon at Blue Hill, Woodson, J.
After winning a scholarship to an academically challenging boarding school, Maizon finds herself one of only five black students there and wonders if she will ever fit in.
Ages 10-up, Grade levels 5-up
ISBN: 0385307969

Make a Joyful Sound,
Poems explore African American history, identity, culture, as well as universal themes in a life-affirming manner.
ISBN: 1-56288-000-4

Malcolm X, Adoff, A.
Ages 3-6, Grade levels Pre-K-3
ISBN: 069051414X

Many Thousand Gone, Fair, Ronald
A sequel to *The People Could Fly*, this volume tells the stories of those who escaped the Holocaust of African Enslavement and those who had to summon the courage to fight it in other ways.
All ages, All grades
ISBN: 0-394-92873-2

Mariah Keeps Cool, Pitts, Mildred
Mariah spends a wonderful, exciting summer with family and friends.
Ages 8-12, Grade levels 3-7
ISBN: 0-02-792295-2

Mariah Loves Rock, Pitts, Mildred
When 11-year-old Mariah learns that her half-sister is to become part of her close-knit family, she adds this to her current list of worries including another sister she finds "weird", and her own a crush on a rock star.
Grade levels 3 - 7
ISBN: 0-8167-1838-5

Marindy and Brother Wind, McKissack, Patricia
Ages 3-8, Grade levels Pre-K-3

Marked By Fire, Thomas, J
ISBN: 0-380-79327-X

Martin Luther King, McKissack, Patricia
This book addresses King's relationship with other
black leaders, movements, politicians, and the
FBI, as well as allegations of his Communist views.
Grade levels 2-3
ISBN: 0894903020

Martin Luther King, The Peaceful Warrior
Clayton, Edward
A biography of the black leader who tried to achieve
equality for his race through nonviolent methods.
ISBN: 0-671-73242-0

Mary Had a Little Lamb, Hale, Sarah Josepha
Ages 3-8, Grade levels Pre-K-3
ISBN: 0590437739

Mary Jo's Grandmother, Udry, Janice May
Whenever Mary Jo selected something to "show
and tell," her classmates had already chosen it.
Finally she brought a very special person to share
with her class.
Ages 8-9, Grade levels 3-4
ISBN: 0-8075-4984-3

Mary McLeod Bethune, Greenfield, Eloise
Simple story of the black woman who became the
great educator and inspiration of black children.
"I leave you faith, I leave you love."
Grade levels K-4
ISBN: 0516042556

Matthew and Tilly, Jones, Rebecca
An African American girl and a white boy are friends
in an Eastern city neighborhood when they have a
disagreement. In the end they resolve their
argument and become friends again.
Ages 4-7, Grade levels K-2
ISBN: 0525446842

The Great Hamilton, M. C. Higgins, Virginia
Higgins dreams of saving his family's home from the
slag heap. But it is not until two strangers enter his
life that he learns the answer to his dreams lies in
coming to terms with his family heritage and his
own identity.
Ages 12-up, Grade levels 7-up,
ISBN: 0020434901

Me Day, Lexau, Joan M.
"Daddy said slowly, "Look, your mother and me are
divorced. Not you kids, no way! You and me
are tight, Buddy." Rafer's birthday turns out to be
the best day ever.
Grade levels K-3

Me & Neesie, Greenfield, Eloise
Neesie is the free spirited, make-believe friend of
Janell. But when Janell begins school, she's not
sure she needs Nessie any more.
Ages 5-8, Grade levels K-3
ISBN: 0-690-00715-9

Me, Mop and the Moondance Kid,
Myers, Walter, Dean
T. J. and his younger brother, Moondance, have just
been adopted and hope to get MOP (Miss Olivia
Parrish) adopted while turning their Little League
team into a winner.
Ages 8-12, Grade levels 3-7
ISBN: 0440500656

Meantime, MacKinnon, Bernie
A black family finds life in a middle-class suburb full
of trials as they try to cope with the hostility
of their white neighbors and classmates.
Ages 12-up, Grade levels 7-up
ISBN: 0-395-61622-0

Messy Bessey's Closet, McKissack, Patricia
ISBN: 0-516-02091-9

Messy Bessey's Garden, McKissack, Patricia
Messy Bessey discovers that with proper care her
garden will flourish. From the Rookie Reader
series.
Ages 5-7, Grade levels K-2
ISBN: 0516020080

Meet Addy, Porter, C.
Ages 3-8, Grade levels Pre-K-3
ISBN: 1-56247-076-0

Middle of Somewhere,
Nine-year-old Rebecca and her family, living in a South African village of black Africans, are threatened with forced removal to a bleak, distant development, to make room for a new suburb for whites. Rebecca comes to realize how much her home means to her and her family.
Ages 13-up, Grade levels 8-up
ISBN: 0531085082

Millicent's Ghost, Lexau, Joan M.
Grade levels K-3

(A) Million Fish...More or Less,
Set in Southern Louisiana, a young boy learns how to fish from his elders with extraordinary results.
Ages 7-9, Grade levels 2-4
ISBN: 0679906924

Miranda & Brother Wind, McKissack, Patricia
A young girl dreams of winning a dance contest. She asks the elusive Brother Wind for help.
Ages 5-8, Grade levels K-3,
ISBN: 0394887654

Mississippi Bridge, Taylor, Mildred D.
A ten-year-old white boy is bewildered by the treatment of blacks in 1930s rural Mississippi. One tragic incident serves to prove to him that all people are the same.
Ages 12-15, Grade levels 7-10,
ISBN: 0-8037-0427-5

Mojo Means One, Feelings, M.
Grade levels K-3
ISBN: 0-8037-5711-5

Monkey-Monkey's Trick, McKissack, Patricia
ISBN: 0394991737

Moon Jumpers, Udry, Janice May
Ages 6-7, Grade levels 1-2
ISBN: 0-06-026145-5

Mop, Moondance and the Nagasaki Knights, Myers, Walter Dean
The sequel to *Me, Mop, and the Moondance Kid*, finds Mop and Moondance adopted and out to lead their team to victory over the Nagasaki baseball team and help a homeless youngster.
Ages 8-12, Grade levels 3-7

More Stories Julian Tells, Cameron, Ann
Julian tells some very funny tall tales.
For older readers
ISBN: 0394969693

More Tales of Uncle Remus, Lester, Julius
This companion volume to *The Tales of Uncle Remus: The Adventures of Brer Rabbit* includes retelling the thirty-seven stories from Joel Chandler Harris' compilation of African American animal fables.
ISBN: 0803704208

Motown And Didi: A Love Story.
Myers, Walter Dean
Didi is intent on escaping her stress-ridden life in Harlem by attending college across the country.
ISBN: 0-440-95762-1

Mountain Men, Miller, R.
Join black trailblazer Jim Beckworth as he journeyed through the Sierra Nevada mountains, or trade furs with Jean Batiste DuSable, the founder of the city of Chicago.
Ages 9-12, Grade levels 4-7
ISBN: 0-382-24082-0

Mouse Rap, Myers, Walter Dean
For 14-year-old Mouse, the summer is anything but boring. His father, who left the family 8 years ago, wants to come back as his dad; he has a new girlfriend from California who seems crazy about him, and there is a rumor that there is lots of money to be found somewhere in the neighborhood from a hidden 1930s bank robber.
Ages 12-16, Grade levels 7-11
ISBN: 0060243449

Moves Make the Man, Brooks, Bruce
A black basketball player and a troubled white team mate form an interesting and special friendship.
Ages 12-15, Grade levels 7-10
ISBN: 0064470229

Mr. Kelso Lion, Bontemps, Arna
Because of zoning ordinances, life for people in a small Alabama town is made miserable by a lion that is boarded there. Percy and his grandfather, visitors to the town, confront local governmental agencies with success.
Ages 8-9, Grade levels 3-4

Mr. Monkey & the Gocha Bush,
Myers, Walter Dean

Mufaro's Beautiful Daughters, Steptoe, J.
ISBN: 0688129358

The Music Maker, Guy, R.

Music of Summer,
When Sarah, a dark skinned African American, visits her more affluent and lighter skinned cousin on Cape Cod, she discovers a sense of pride and direction from what turns an ugly summer into a bright awakening.
Ages 12-up, Grade levels 7-up
ISBN: 0-385-305990

My Brother Fine with Me, Clifton, Lucille
An eight-year-old girl gladly helps her nuisance five-year-old brother pack when he decides to leave home. However, when he is gone, the house is too quiet, she is restless and has nobody to play with. She looks outside and is delighted to find him sitting on the front steps.
Ages 4-5, Grade levels Pre-K-K
ISBN: 0-03-014171-0

My Doll, Keshia, Greenfield, Eloise
A board book in which a little girl talks about her special friend, a doll named Keshia.
Ages 2-5, Grade levels Pre-K-K
ISBN: 0-86316-203-7

My First Kwanzaa Book, Newton, Deborah M.
Introduces Kwanzaa, the holiday in which African Americans celebrate their cultural heritage.
Grade levels 1-2
ISBN: 0-590-45762-4

My Friend Jacob, Clifton, Lucille
Warm friendship is celebrated between eight-year-old Sam and sixteen-year-old Jacob, a retarded youth who lives next door.
Ages 8-9, Grade levels 3-4
ISBN: 0-525-35487-5

My Grandpa and the Sea, Orr, Katherine
Story of a boy on a Caribbean Island whose grandfather loses his livelihood as a fisherman, but triumphs through his independence and strong will to build a new and unique career.
Ages 4-5, Grade level K
ISBN: 0876144091

My Little Island, Lessac, F.
ISBN: 0064431460

My Mama Needs Me, Walter, Mildred Pitts
Jason wants to help, but isn't sure that his mother needs him at all after she brings home a new baby from the hospital.
Grade levels 2-3
ISBN: 0688016715

My Name Is Not Angelica, O'Dell, Scott
Captured in Africa and transported to St. John Island, sixteen-year-old Raisha becomes a house enslaved African named Angelica, who risks her life to help the other enslaved Africans.
Ages 14-17, Grade levels 9-12
ISBN: 0395510619

My Special Best Words, Steptoe, J.
ISBN: 0-670-50118-2

My Soul Looks Back in Wonder (Poetry),
Feelings, T.
ISBN: 0-8037-1001-1

My Soul's High Song, Cullen, Countee
This is the only modern collection of the body of
work produced by perhaps the 20th century's
greatest poet, and his name is absolutely
obscure...buy this, read this and teach this man!
ISBN: 0-385-41295-9

Mystery of Dream House, Hamilton, Virginia
A masterfully crafted sequel to *The House of Dies
Drear* that picks up the story of the Small family and
the dilemmas that must be resolved upon the
discovery of the long-dead abolitionist's hidden
treasure.
Ages 12-up, Grade levels 7-up
ISBN: 0020434804

Mystery at the Zoo, Supraner, Robyn
Little boy wonders what has happened to his favorite
lion who has escaped from the zoo.
Ages 5-7, Grade levels K-2
ISBN: 0893750794

Naja the Snake and Mangus the Mongoose,
Kirkpatrick, Oliver

Nathaniel's Talking, Greenfield, Eloise
Nine-year-old Nathaniel makes clear his philosophy
and impressions of life in a poetry collection that
covers joy, grief, and the future.
Ages 8-10, Grade levels 3-5
ISBN: 0-86316-200-2

Nat Turner, Bisson, Terry
This book is a biography of the enslaved African
whose unsuccessful rebellion was one of the
events that paved the way for the abolition of the
holocaust of African enslavement.
Grade levels 6-7
ISBN: 1555466133

Nelson Mandela, McKissack, Patricia

Nettie Jo's Friends, McKissack, Patricia
Nettie Jo can't go to her cousin's wedding unless
she leaves her tattered doll at home. Nettie decides
to make her a new dress and sets out to find a
needle and cloth for the job.
Ages 4-7, Grade levels K-2,
ISBN: 0394891589

New Guys Around the Block, Guy, R.
ISBN: 0-440-95888-1

Night of the Ghosts and Hermits, Stolz, Mary
Nocturnal life on the seashore.
ISBN: 015257333X

Night on Neighborhood Street, Greenfield, Eloise
Beautifully illustrated book of poetry expressing the
heart warming and loving atmosphere of family.
Ages 5-up, Grade levels K-up
ISBN: 0803707789

Nini at Carnival, Lloyd Errol
ISBN: 0-690038925

Nobody's Family Is Going to Change,
Eleven-year-old Emma wants to become a lawyer,
but her father wants her brother Willie to become
the lawyer. Willie wants to be a dancer. Book
examines women's rights, children's rights and
inter-family relationships.
Ages 10-14, Grade levels 5-9
ISBN: 0-374-45523-6

The Noonday Friends

Not So Fast Songololo
Small African boy goes shopping in town with his
grandmother. She is made nervous by the traffic
and crowds and he is excited by everything.
Ages 4-7, Grade levels K-2
ISBN: 0140507159

Not Yet, Yvette, Ketteman, H.
Ages 3-8, Grade levels Pre-K-3
ISBN: 0807557714

Now Is Your Time, Myers, Walter Dean
Tells the story of many men and women, from captured, enslaved Africans to their present day descendants, whose work, inventiveness, and courage forever changed the direction of life in America.
Ages 11-up, Grade levels 6-up
ISBN: 0-06-024371-6; 0-06-446120-3

Oh Brother, Wilson, Jonnice
The story of two very different brothers and how one decided to "educate" the other.
Ages 10-12, Grade levels 5-7
ISBN: 0-590-410016

Oh Kojo, How Could You? Verna, Aardema
Kojo is always being tricked out of his mother's money by Ananse until one day, he fools the trickster.
Ages 4-7, Grade levels K-2
ISBN: 0-8037-0007-5

One More River to Cross, Haskin
The stories of 12 African Americans who have made major contributions to American life.
Ages 12-16, Grade levels 7-11
ISBN: 0590428969

One Smiling Grandma, Linden, A.
Ages 3-8. Grade levels Pre-K-3
ISBN: 0803711328

One of Three, Johnson,
A little girl discovers the reality of being the youngest when her two older sisters no longer want her to tag along.
Ages 3-6, Grade levels Pre-K-1
ISBN: 0531085554

The Orphan Boy, Mollel, T.
ISBN: 0899199852

Out from This Place, Hansen, Joyce
Grade levels 6-7
ISBN: 0802768172

Outside Shot, Myers, Walter Dean
ISBN: 0440967848

Paris, Pee Wee, and Big Dog, Guy, Rosa
ISBN: 04404400724

The Party, Johnson, S.

Pass It On: African American Poetry for Children, Hudson, W.
A beautifully illustrated collection of poetry by such African American poets as Langston Hughes, Nikki Giovanni, Eloise Greenfield, and Lucille Clifton.
Ages 5- 1, Grade levels K-6
ISBN: 0590457705

Patchwork Quilt, Flournoy, Valerie
A grandmother's devotion to the making of her last quilt is carried on by her granddaughter and daughter.
Ages 5-9, Grade levels K-3
ISBN: 0-8037-0098-9

Paul Lawrence Dunbar, McKissack, Patricia
This book presents a turn-of-the-century black poet and novelist whose works were among the first to give an honest presentation of black life.
Grade levels 6-7

Paul Robeson, Greenfield, Eloise
This biography of a great singer emphasizes his role as a political activist and covers the major points of his childhood.
Grade levels 3-4
ISBN: 0690006608

People Could Fly, Hamilton, Virginia
An anthology of African American folktales collected by Virginia Hamilton.
Ages 5-12, Grade levels K-7
ISBN: 0394969251

People Could Fly/Cassette, Hamilton, Virginia
An anthology of African American folktales. The cassette features the voices of author Virginia Hamilton and actor James Earl Jones.
 All ages, All grades,
ISBN: 0-394-96925-1; 0-679-84336-1

Petey Moroni's Camp Runamok Diary,
Cummings, Pat
A group of young campers try to figure out why their
food keeps disappearing.
Ages 5-8, Grade levels K-3
ISBN: 0027255131

Phillip Hall Likes Me. I Reckon Maybe,
Green Bette
Eleven-year-old Beth, a lively Black girl, thinks that
Philip Hall likes her, but their on-again, off-again
relationship sometimes makes her wonder.
Ages 10-11, Grade levels 5-6
ISBN: 1-55736-106-1

Phoebe and the General, Griffin, Judith
The thirteen-year-old daughter of a free black
businessman in New York City is sent to serve as a
housekeeper for General George Washington. While
serving the General, she prevents a murder
attempt on his life.
Grade levels 4-6
ISBN: 0698306295

Phoebe the Spy, Griffin, Judith
A free black man and his daughter help General
George Washington during the American Revolution.
Ages 8-11, Grade levels 3-6
ISBN: 0-590-05758-8

The Picture Life of Malcolm X, Haskins, James
ISBN: 0-531-02771-6

The Picture Book of Martin Luther King, Jr.,
Adler, David A.
A brief, illustrated, biography of the Baptist minister
and civil rights leader whose philosophy and
practice of nonviolent civil disobedience helped
African Americans win many battles for equal
rights.
ISBN: 0-8234-0770-5; 0-8234-0847-7

Picture Life of Martin Luther King Jr.,
Young, Margaret
This easy-to-read biography, which is enhanced with
numerous photographs, highlights King's life.
Ages 8-9, Grade levels 3-4

Pioneers, Sandle,
Readers will find out about the black role in the
California gold rush; learn about Biddy Mason, a
former enslaved African turned landowner, and ride
with George Monroe for the Pony Express.
Ages 9-12, Grade levels 4-7
ISBN: 006023024X

Plain City, Hamilton, Virginia
Grade levels 7-11
ISBN: 0590473646

Planet of Junior Brown, Hamilton, Virginia
Two outcast boys discover a world of their own in
the basement of their New York City school.
Ages 12-up, Grade levels 7-up
ISBN: 0-8161-4262-X

Pocket for Corduroy, Freeman, Don
While in the laundromat with Lisa and her mother,
Corduroy the bear realizes that he does not have a
pocket on his overalls.
Grade levels K-3
ISBN: 067056172

Poor Girl, Rich Girl, Wilson, Jeannice
Grade levels 7-9
ISBN: 0590447327

Pretend You're a Cat, Marzollo, Jean
A multicultural book for preschoolers in which the
children pretend they can make all the moves
and sounds of a cat.
Ages 2-4, Grade levels Pre-K-K
ISBN: 0803707746

The Prince, Johnson, S.

Princess Gorilla and a New Kind of Water,
Aardema, Verna
ISBN: 0-8037-0413-5

Princess of the Full Moon, Guirma, Frederic
Tales of Mogho; African Stories from Upper Volta.

Quentin Corn, Stolz, Mary
Ages 8-9, Grade levels 3-4
ISBN: 1-56790-024-1

The Quilt, Jonas, Ann
A child discovers the world of her imagination as she studies her patch-work quilt made from many things she has outgrown.
Ages 4-9, Grade levels K-4
ISBN: 0688038255

Rabbit Makes A Monkey Out Of Lion,
Aardama, Verna
Beautifully illustrated by award-winner Jerry Pinkney, this is the story of a smart and nimble Rabbit who makes a fool of the mighty King of the forest.
Ages 4-8, Grade levels K-3
ISBN: 0803702981

Ragtime Tumpie, Schroeder, Alan
A slice of the colorful history of American jazz and the young dreams of ragtime dancer Josephine Baker, also known as Ragtime Tumpie.
Ages 6-8, Grade levels 1-3
ISBN: 0-316-77504-5

Rainbabies, Laura, Melmed
A childless couple receives 12 times their hearts desire during the magic of a moonshower! 12 tiny little babies, who are small enough to rock to sleep in a wooden shoe! This is a classic folktale!
All ages, All grades
ISBN: 0688107567

Ray Charles, Mathis, Sharon Bell
This is a short biography of the black jazz musician from his impoverished childhood to success despite obstacles, including blindness.
Grade levels 7-8
ISBN: 0791020800

The Real McCoy, The Life Of An African-American Inventor, Towle, W.
A biography of a Canadian-born African American who studied in Scotland and patented over fifty inventions despite obstacles he faced because of his race.
Ages 8-12, Grade levels 3-7
ISBN: 0-590-43596-5

Red Dog, Blue Fly, Mathis, Sharon
A book of poetry for even "tough little boys," includes such situations as being yelled at by the coach, learning football plays, and having a girl on the team.
Ages 7-12, Grade levels 2-7
ISBN: 0670836230

Reflections of a Black Cowboy (Set of 4),
Miller, Robert
These books highlight the often forgotten contributions of famous African Americans who played vital roles in taming the Wild West.
Ages 9-12, Grade levels 4-7
ISBN: 0382240804 ISBN: 0382240820

Righteous Revenge of Artemis Bonner,
Myers, Walter Dean
A funny Western novel which follows the exploits of 15-year-old Artemis, who journeys from New York City to Tombstone, Arizona, in 1882, to avenge the murder of his uncle.
Ages 10-14, Grade levels 5-9
ISBN: 0060208465

River That Gave Gifts, Humphrey, Margo
Stories and pictures by African American artist Margo Humphrey, "River" tells the adventures of Yanava, a beautiful dark brown child who creates a special gift for her grandmother.
Ages 7-12, Grade levels 2-7
ISBN: 0892390271

Road to Memphis, Taylor, Mildred D.
1991 Coretta Scott King Award.
In rural 1941 Mississippi, Cassie Logan becomes caught up in a world of prejudice and racial tension.
Ages 14-Y. A., Grade 9-up
ISBN: 0803703406

Robin on His Own, Wilson, Johnniece
A boy struggles to come to terms with the grief and changes that accompany the death of his mother.
ISBN: 0590418130

Roll of Thunder, Hear My Cry, Taylor, Mildred D.
A black family living in the South during the 1930s is faced with prejudice and discrimination which their children don't understand.
Ages 10-14, Grade levels 5-8
ISBN: 0803774737

Rosa Parks, Greenfield, Eloise
This biography of Rosa Parks focuses on her role in precipitating the 1955 Montgomery, Alabama Bus Boycott.
Ages 8-9, Grade levels 3-4,
ISBN: 0-690-71211-1

Rose for Abby, Guthrie, Donna
Abby lives in the city and her neighborhood has many homeless people. Abby comes up with creative ways to help the homeless in her area.
Ages 5-8, Grade levels K-3
ISBN: 0-687-36586-4

The Rough Face Girl, Martin, Rafe
Every girl wants to marry this fine warrior, but Rough Face is the only one who has the knowledge to do so! Her face is charred from tending the fires...will she win this handsome man?
Ages 6-12, Grade levels 1-6
ISBN: 0399218599

Runaway to Freedom, A Story of the Underground Railway, Smucker, Barbara
Two young enslaved African girls escape from a plantation in Mississippi and find a hazardous route toward freedom in Canada via the Underground Railroad.
Ages 10-11, Grade levels 5-6
ISBN: 0-06-440106-5

Saddle Club,
One in a series of 26 stories which follow the lives of Stevie, Carol and Lisa, three very different African American girls who love horses and are best friends at the Pine Hollo Stables.
Ages 9-11, Grade levels 4-6
ISBN: 0-553-15983-6

Sam Patch, the High, Wide, and Handsome Jumper, Bontemps, Arna
This retelling of the Sam Patch legend shows him growing up and learning to take bigger and better jumps until he defeats Hurricane Harry, the snapping turtle who boasted that he was the best jumper of all times.

Samuel's Choice, Berieth, Richard
A fourteen-year-old enslaved African tries to decide with whom to fight during the American Revolution.
Ages 8-11, Grade levels 3-6,
ISBN: 0-8075-7218-7

Say It Again, Granny, Aagard, John
ISBN: 0-370-30676-7

School Bus, Crews, Donald
Ages 3-8, Grade levels Pre-k-3
ISBN: 0-688-02807-1

Scorpions, Myers, Walter Dean
Twelve-year-old friends live in Harlem and are confronted with the "choice" to join The Scorpions, a gang. Jamal, who is black, raises money for his imprisoned brother's legal fees by running crack for the gang. The gun which he inherits as gang leader is used by his Puerto Rican friend, Tito, to save Jamal's life. This story of a cold and frightening world has a barely comforting ending.
Grade levels 5-9
ISBN: 0060243651

Secret of Gumbo Grove, Tate, Eleanora E.
While helping to clean the town's old cemetery, Raisin Stackhouse becomes involved in a search for some local black history that many of the town's residents would just as soon forget.
Ages 10-13, Grade levels 5-7
ISBN: 0553272268

Seven Candles for Kwanzaa, Pinkney, A. D.
Highlights the seven days of Kwanzaa as each candle is lighted.
ISBN: 0803712936

Shadow, Brown, Marcia
Shadow lives in the forest and comes out at night to prowl the fires and join the dancers around the camp fires.
All ages, All grades,
ISBN: 0689710844

Shake It to the One You Love the Best, Maddox, C.
Ages Pre K-8, Grade levels K-3
ISBN: 0962338109

Shawn Goes to School, Breinburg, Petronella
Shawn has always wanted to go to school, but when the big day comes he panics and cries. Comfort and support from a kind teacher, his mother, and an older sister ease his fears.
Ages 4-5, Grade levels Pre-K-K
ISBN: 0-690-00277-7

Shawn's Red Bike, Breinburg, Petronella
Ages 4-5, Grade levels Pre-K-K

She Come Bringing Me That Little Baby Girl, Greenfield, Eloise
When Kevin sees his infant sister for the first time, his is downright disturbed at the adults' responses to her. His Uncle Ray helps him to appreciate his big brother role.
Grade Level K-2
ISBN: 0-397-31586-4

She Wanted to Read, Greenfield, Eloise
The story of Mary McLeod Bethune's childhood and her wonderful rise to greatness.
NO ISBN

Shimmershine Queens, Yarbrough, Camille
Ten-year-old Angie is teased about her dark skin and kinky hair and worries about her parents' separation until a friend helps her find the "shimmershine" feeling that makes her feel good about herself.
Ages 10-13, Grade levels 5-8
ISBN: 0399214658

Shortcut, Crews, Donald
Children taking a shortcut along a railroad track find danger when a train approaches.
Ages 3-8, Grade levels Pre-K-3
ISBN: 068806437X

Side walk Story, Mathis, Sharon Bell
When her best friend's family is evicted from their apartment, a nine-year-old girl decides to do something about the situation.
Ages 7-10, Grade levels 2-5
ISBN: 0-14-032165-9

Sing to the Sun, Ashley, Bryan
You will remember the author as the winner of the Coretta Scott King award for 1992 with his stunning book of African American spirituals for children, *All Day, All Night*. This is Ashley's first book for children.
Grade levels 2-6
ISBN: 0060208333

Singing Tales of Africa, Robinson, Adjai

Siri The Conquistador, Stolz, Mary
Ages 8-9, Grade levels 3-4
NO ISBN

Sister, Greenfield, Eloise
Tells the story of Doretha, a confused thirteen year old who tries to find herself in her own words, written during the past four years in her diary.
Ages 10-13, Grade levels 5-8
ISBN: 0-690-0049704; 0-06-440199-5

They Showed the Way, Forty American Negro Leaders, Rollins, Charlemae
Biographical accounts are presented of blacks successful in a wide variety of careers, ranging from the creative arts to the professions of law and medicine, exploration and invention, publishing, and religion.

Sky Man, Johnson, S.
Grade levels 2 - 3
ISBN: 0-553-29723-6

The Slave Dancer, Fox, Paula
In this story set in 1840, slave ship traders kidnap 13-year-old Jessie and force him to "dance the slaves" by playing his fife while they exercise.
Ages 10-11, Grade levels 5-6
ISBN: 0-02-735560-8

A Snowy Day, Keats, Jack
Peter awoke to find high snowdrifts outside his window and went out to play in this beautiful white world.
Ages 4-8, Grade levels Pre-K-3
ISBN: 0-670-65400-0; 0-14-050182-7

Sojourner Truth, Slave, Abolitionist, Fighter for Women's Rights, Lindstrom, Aletha
The biography of a former enslaved African who became one of the best-known abolitionists of her day and spent her life trying to improve living conditions for African Americans.
Grade levels 5-6
ISBN: 0-671-32988-X

Solomon's Secret, Pirotta, Savior
ISBN: 0803706944

Some of the Days of Everett Anderson,
Clifton, Lucille
Chronicles the daily activities of Everett Anderson.
Grade levels 3-4
ISBN: 0-8050-0290-1

Something on My Mind, Nikki Grimes
A collection of poems that expresses the hopes, fears, joys, and sorrows of growing up.
Ages 6-8, Grade levels 1-3

Something to Count on, Moore, E.
ISBN: 0-525-39595-4

Somewhere in the Darkness, Myers, Walter Dean
Myers never misses the gold. This is his latest novel, and it touches a sensitive issue between a young African American male who has not seen his father since he was three years old. When he comes home late one evening, he hears a voice calling his name...who could that be? Read about what happens when he encounters his father.
Grade levels 7-11
ISBN: 0590424114

Songs and Stories from Uganda,
Serwadda, William
ISBN: 0-937203-157

Song of The Trees, Taylor, Mildred D.
Cassie loves the forest around her home and believes they sing. She fears for them when her grandmother is tricked into selling them.
Ages 1011, Grade levels 5-6,
ISBN: 0-8037-5452-3

The Soul of Christmas, King, Helen Hayes
A black family in the city prepares to celebrate Christmas.
Ages 8-9, Grade levels 3-4
ISBN: 0-87485-057-6

South, North, East and West, Edited by Michael Rosen with a foreword by Whoopi Goldberg
Tales from Brazil, Greece, Jamaica, and Vietnam are just a few of the selections from this volume of 25 stories. This book was written to benefit the Oxfam self-help projects around the world!
All ages, All grades

South Town, Graham, Lorenz
This is a sequel to *South Town and North Town*. David Williams, eighteen, is in conflict about the best stance for African Americans as he experiences discrimination and is torn between the moderate path and that advocated by a Black Power figure.
Ages 10-11, Grade levels 5-6
ISBN: 0-382-24854-6

Spin a Soft Black Song, Giovanni, Nikki
These poems are about black children on the themes of mommies, daddies, babies, haircuts, basketball, and dreams.
Grade levels 3-4
ISBN: 0-374-46469-3

Sport Pages, Adolph, A.

Stevie, Steptoe, John
A child resents, and then misses, a little foster brother.
Ages 6-8, Grade levels 1-3
ISBN: 0-06-025764-4

Sticks and Stones, Bobbie Bones, Roberts, A
ISBN: 0-590-46518-X

Stories Julian Tells, Cameron, Ann
Julian loves to tell stories, especially to delight his younger brother. But this time Julian tells a story that gets the two boys into a lot of trouble.
Ages 7-9, Grade levels 2-4
ISBN: 0-394-94301-5

Storm in the Night, Stolz, Mary
A stormy night is the perfect time for Thomas to listen to the stories of his grandfather's childhood.
Ages 5-8, Grade levels K-3
ISBN: 0-06-025913-2

Story of The Jumping Mouse, Steptoe, John
Retelling of a Native American folktale by African-American writer and illustrator, John Steptoe.

Story of the Negro, Bontemps, Arna
This history of blacks from the days of antiquity provides a chronology of events from 1700 B.C. with comparable dates in world history.

Striped Ice Cream, Lexau, Joan M.
Ages 8-9, Grade levels 3-4
ISBN: 0-397-31047-1

Sukey and the Mermaid, San Souci, Robert D.
Unhappy with her life at home on the Sea Island off the South Carolina coast, Sukey finds her wishes answered by goodness and love as taught by a mermaid.
Ages 5-8, Grade levels K-3
ISBN: 0027781410

Summer Wheels, Bunting, Eve
The bicycle man fixes up old bicycles and offers both his friendship and the use of the bikes to the multi-ethnic neighborhood kids.
Ages 6-10, Grade levels 1-5
ISBN: 0152070001

Sundiata: Lion King of Mali,
Beautifully illustrated, true story about Sundiata, who overcame physical handicaps and strong opposition to rule Mali in the thirteenth century.
Ages 8-12, Grade levels 3-7
ISBN: 0395613027

The Sunflower Garden, Udry, May Janice
Ages 8-9, Grade levels 3-4

Susannah and the Blue House Mystery, Elmore, P.
ISBN: 0-525-40525-9

Susannah and the Poison Green Halloween,
Elmore, P
ISBN: 0-590-43471-3

Susannah and the Purple Mongoose Mystery,
Elmore, P.
ISBN: 0-525-44907-8

Sweet Clara and the Freedom Quilt,
Hopkinson, Deborah
A young girl stitches a quilt with a map pattern which guides her to freedom in the North.
Ages 6-12, Grade levels 1-7,
ISBN: 0-679-92311-X

Sweet Whispers, Brothers Rush, Hamilton, Virginia
Grade levels 7-8
ISBN: 0399208941

T for Tommy, Lexau, Joan M.
Ages 4-5, Grade levels Pre-K-K
ISBN: 0-8116-6719-7

Tailypo, Wahi, J.
Grade levels 3-4
ISBN: 0805006877

Take a Walk in Their Shoes, Turner, Glennette Tiley
How unusual, 14 biographies of African Americans like Madame Walker, Arthur Schomburg, and Oscar Micheaux are included with a short skit at the end for use in classroom or for church plays. When putting on a drama skit...this is it!
Grade levels 4-8
ISBN: 0-525-65006-7

Tales of Mogho, Guirma, Frederic
African stories from Upper Volta.

The Tales of Uncle Remus, Lester, Julius
Describes the adventures of Brer Rabbit and Brer Fox's tricks and encounters with Brother Man.
Ages 8-10, Grade levels 3-5
ISBN: 0803702728

Talk About a Family, Greenfield, Eloise
This book views a young girl's experience when parental strife disrupts her family. A neighbor helps her to understand that broken things can assume new shapes and be made to work again.
Grade levels 3-4
ISBN: 0397325045

Talk That Talk, Gross & Barnes
Anthology of African American folktales.
All ages, All grades,
ISBN: 0-671-67168-5

Talking Eggs, San Souci, Robert D.
An adaptation of a Creole folktale, two sisters, one kind, the other selfish, are tested by an old woman who rewards the most generous.
Ages 5-8, Grade levels K-3,
ISBN: 0-8037-0619-7

The Talking Tree, Baker, Augusta
Fairy tales from fifteen different lands. This collection represents choices of young listeners at the New York Public Library's story hours. Each story is characteristic of the culture it represents.

Talking with Artist, Cummings, Pat (Editor)
14 children's books illustrators talk to kids and parents about their work, their childhood, how they got started. It includes a childhood picture of each artist and samples of their work! A great inspirational too!
ISBN: 0027242455

Tancy, Hurmence, Belinda
At the end of the Civil War, a young house-enslaved African in North Carolina, Tancy, searches for her mother, who was sold when she was a baby.
Ages 11-14, Grade levels 6-9
ISBN: 0-89919-228-9

Tar Beach, Ringgold, Faith
African American artist Faith Ringgold remembers how her family spent their summer days on the roof of their New York apartment building, sunning themselves and daydreaming on "tar beach."
Ages 7-12, Grade levels 2-7
ISBN: 0-517-58031-4

Taste of Salt, Temple, F.
ISBN: 0-531-08609-7

Teammates, Golenbock, Peter
Describes the racial prejudice experienced by Jackie Robinson when he joined the Brooklyn Dodgers and became the first black player in major league baseball. Also depicts the support he received from white teammate Pee Wee Reese.
Grade levels 2-6
ISBN: 0-15-200603-6

Tell Me a Story Mama, Johnson, Angela
A mother and preschool-aged daughter get ready for bed with stories of mother's childhood.
Ages 3-7, Grade levels Pre-K-2
ISBN: 0531083942

Ten Black Dots, Crews, Donald
Objects from one to ten are introduced with colors and textures for visual variety.
For older readers
ISBN: 0-688-06068-4

Ten, Nine, Eight, Molly Bang
A father gets his daughter ready for bed with this delightful counting game.
Ages 2-5, Grade levels Pre-K-K
ISBN: 0-688-00906-9

The Test, Johnson, S.
Taken from a traditional nursery rhyme, a child finds a key which lets her escape the harsh city to a magical kingdom filled with color, excitement and love. A beautiful ending says the magical kingdom can be had in real life.
Ages 3-7, Grade levels Pre-K-2

Thank You, Jackie Robinson, Cohen, Barbara
Ten-year-old Sam Green, a skinny Jewish kid, and Davy, an old black man who cooks in Mrs. Green's Inn, share a passion for the Dodgers and Jackie Robinson.
Ages 10-11, Grade levels 5-6
ISBN: 0-590-42378-9

Themba, Sacks, M.
ISBN: 0525674144

The Third Gift, Carew, Jan
This story tells of the Jubas and how their prophet Amakosa brings them to Nameless Mountain where they receive, in time, the gifts of work, beauty, and imagination.
Ages 6-7, Grade levels 1-2
ISBN: 0-316-12847-3

Things I Like About Grandma, Haskins, Francine
"I love to ride the bus with Grandma when she goes to cash her social security check..." It is probably the best line in the entire book! It is realistic reminiscence of spending time with a special loved one, and the bright colors set in caricature form is really appealing. A Children's Press Book.
Grade levels Prek-2
ISBN: 0-89239-107-3

Thief in the Village, Berry, J.
A collection of nine stories, written in the local idiom of a Caribbean village, tells vivid stories of what village life is like.

Ages 1 and up, Grade levels Pre K - up
ISBN: 0-14-034357-1

This is the Key to the Kingdom, Allison, Diane
Grade level Pre-K-3
ISBN: 0316034320

This Strange New Feeling, Lester, Julius
Based on fact, this book looks at Holocaust of African Enslavement and freedom from the lives of three couples.
For older children
ISBN: 0-590-44047-0

Three African Tales, Robinson, Adjai
ISBN: 0-399-20656-6

Three Wishes, Clifton, Lucille
When they find a lucky coin, two friends find that having a good friend is the best kind of luck.
Ages 5-8, Grade levels K-3
ISBN: 0-670-71063-6

Tickle Tickle
ISBN: 0-02-769020-2

Tituba of Salem, Petry, A.
ISBN: 0-690-04766-5

To Be a Slave, Lester, Julius
A collection of first-person interviews with former enslaved Africans right after the Civil War.
Ages 11-16, Grade levels 6-11
ISBN: 0803789556

Together, George, Ella Lym
An African American girl and a white girl celebrate in verse their friendship and togetherness.
Ages 3-6, Grade levels Pre-K-1
ISBN: 0-531-08431-0

To Hell with Dying, Walker, Alice
Beautiful illustrations highlight this book about a young girl's memory of Mr. Sweet, and how, though he was often on the verge of the dying, he could be revived by the loving attention that she and her brother gave him. First children's book by Alice Walker.
Ages 8-up, Grade levels 3-up,
ISBN: 0158290750

Tommy Traveler in the World of Black History,
ISBN: 0-86316-211-8

Toning the Sweep, Johnson, Angela
Ages 3-8, Grade levels Pre-K-3
ISBN: 0531086267

Tower to Heaven,
Retold by Ruby Dee, this African folktale tells the story
of Onyankopon, the sky god, and Yaa, an
old woman of the village who angers him. The
villagers decide to build a tower to heaven in order
to talk to the sky god again.
ISBN: 0-8050-1460-8

Train to Lulu's, Howard, Elizabeth
During the 1930s, two young sisters take a nine-hour
train trip from Boston to Baltimore to visit
their Great-aunt Lulu.
Ages 5-7, Grade levels K-2
ISBN: 0027446204

Train Ride, Steptoe, John
Four black boys, wanting something to do, sneak into
a subway train in Brooklyn and ride to Times Square
where they spend their money in a penny arcade and
earn the spanking of their lives upon returning home.
Ages 6- , Grade levels 1-2
ISBN: 0-06-025773-3

Travelling to Kondo, Aardema, Verna
A tale of Nkundo of Zaire.
ISBN: 067990810

Tree of Life, Bash,
This book follows one year in the life of a Baobab tree
in Africa, which many Africans call
"mother," because it provides shelter and food to an
amazing variety of creatures.
Ages 7-10, Grade levels 2-5
ISBN: 0316083054

Trouble's Child, Walter, Mildred Pitts
Martha, almost fifteen and considered marriageable,
realizes that to get the education she desires,
she must leave the remote Louisiana island and the
herb-doctoring midwifery skills that gave her
grandmother the community's respect.
Grade 8-12
ISBN: 0688-04214-7

Truck, Crews, Donald
This picture book follows a truck from its loading
station to its designation as it encounters road signs,
other trucks on the highway, a truck stop, and the
intricate road system.
Grade levels K-3
ISBN: 0688842445

Truth About The Moon,
An African child is told many stories about the moon,
but feels that he still has not learned the truth.
Ages 5-8, Grade levels K-3
ISBN: 0-395-64371-6

Turtle Knows Your Name, Ashley, Bryan
A small boy with a very long and difficult name that
no one can remember finds a turtle who knows
his name. But his problems do not end there. He is
challenged by his grandmother to find out her
name.
Ages 4-7, Grade levels K-2
ISBN: 0689315783

Turtle Watchers, Powell, Patricia
Three sisters on a Caribbean island band together to
protect a nest of leatherback turtle eggs from
poachers and natural enemies.
Ages 12-15, Grade levels 7-10
ISBN: 067084294X

The Twins Strike Back, Flournoy, Valerie
Ages 8-9, Grade levels 3-6
ISBN: 0-940975-51-3

Two & Too Much, Walter, Mildred
Seven-year-old Brandon's attempt to take care of his
two-year-old sister results in one disaster after
another.
Ages 6-9, Grade levels 1-3
ISBN: 0027922901

Two Ways to Count to Ten, Dee, Ruby
A retelling of a traditional African tale in which King Leopard invites all the animals to a spear throwing contest to determine who will marry his daughter and succeed him as King.
Ages 5-8, Grade levels K-3
ISBN: 080500476

Ty's One Man Band, Walter, Mildred Pitts
Ty meets a mysterious man who, using a washboard, comb, spoons, and pail, forms a one-man band.
Ages 4-8, Grade levels Pre-K-3
ISBN: 0027923002

Uncle Jed's Barbershop, Mitchell, M.
Grade 2-5
ISBN: 0671769693

Under the Sunday Tree, Greenfield, Eloise
In a perfect blend of poetry and painting, the special flavor of life in the Bahamas is captured for young readers.
Ages 7-11, Grade levels 2-6
ISBN: 0060222573

Underground Man, Meltzer, M.
ISBN: 0152006176

Ups and Downs of Carl Davis III, Guy, Rosa
ISBN: 0-440-40744-3

The Very Old Man and the Very Young Boy,
How does one get to know so many stories to tell? Well, one day the very young boy keeps growing until he becomes a very old man, and then he understands all too well...

Vingananee and the Tree Toad, Aardema, Verna
A Liberian tale.
ISBN: 0-14-050892-0

Wagon Wheels, Brenner, Barbara
A young African American boy describes the wilderness adventures of his pioneering family in Kansas in the 1870s.
Ages 6-9, Grade levels 3-4,
ISBN: 0-060-206691

People Publishing Group, Inc.

Waiting for the Rain, Gordon, Shelia
Two South African friends, one black and one white, struggle with the realities of apartheid as their races determine their futures and changes in their relationship.
Ages 12-up, Grade levels 6-up,
ISBN: 0553279114

Walk Together Children, Brown, Ashley
African American Spirituals. Presents the music and lyrics of two dozen black spirituals.

War Comes To Willy Freeman,
A young girl struggles to find and free her mother taken by the British during the American Revolutionary War.
Ages 10-13, Grade levels 5-8
ISBN: 0-440-49504-1

Wave in Her Pocket, Lynn, Joseph
Folktales from Trinidad.
Ages 8-12, Grade levels 4-8
ISBN: 0395544327

W. E. B. DuBois: A Biography,
Robinson, Paul, Hamilton, Virginia
Grade levels 7-11
ISBN: 0-690-87256-9

A Weed Is a Flower, The Life of George Washington Carver, Aliki
A biography of the man who was born an enslaved African but lived to become one of America's greatest research scientists.
Ages 6-10, Grade levels 1-5,
ISBN: 0-671-66118-3; 0-671-66490-5

We Keep a Store, Shelby, Anne
A little girl talks about how she and her family enjoy operating a small country store.
Age 4, Grade level Pre-K
ISBN: 0-531-08456-6

We Read: A to Z, Crews, Donald
Alphabet letters are combined with illustrations to provide concepts that children can see and use.
For older headers
ISBN: 0-688-03844-1

1-800-822-1080

West Indian Folk Tales, Sherlock, Sir Philip
ISBN: 0-8446-6658-0

What a Morning!, Langstaff, John
The Christmas Story of Black Spirituals which tell the story of the birth of Christ.
Grade levels 3-4
ISBN: 0-689-50422-5

What Kind of Baby Sitter Is This?, Johnson, D.
A most unusual baby sitter wins over her young charge.
Ages 5-8, Grade levels K-3
ISBN: 0-02-747846-7

What Mary Jo Shared, Udry, Janice May
Shy Mary Jo shares her father at her school's "Show and Tell," reminding everyone of the warmth of family.
Ages 5-7, Grade levels K-2
ISBN: 0-8075-8842-3; 0-590-43757-7

What's So Funny, Ketu?, Aardema, Verna
A hilarious story about a man who was given the "gift" of being able to read animals' minds.
ISBN: 0-8037-0646-4

What Will Mommy Do When I'm at School, Johnson, D.
As she gets ready for her first day in school, a little girl worries about how her mom will fill her time.
Ages 3-6, Grade levels Pre-K-1
ISBN: 0-02-747845-9

When I Am Old with You, Johnson, Angela
A grandchild imagines a time when he is the same age as his grandfather and what they can share together, not realizing that they will never be the same age at the same time.
Ages 4-7, Grade levels K-2

When I Was Little, Igus, Toyomi
Toyomi features a young African American male spending time with his grandfather growing up. This book is published by one of the two African American children's book publishers in the United States.
Grade levels K-4
ISBN: 0-9490975-33-5

When the Rattle Snake Sounds, Childress, Alice
This one-act play, set in a hotel laundry room in Cape May, New Jersey, in the 1860s describes an incident which occurred when Harriet Tubman worked as a laundress to raise money for the abolitionist cause.
ISBN: 0-698-305949

Where Does the Trail Lead?, Burton, Albert
With the smell of the sea always in his nostrils, a boy follows an island path through flowers and pine needles, over the dunes, to a reunion with his family at the edge of the sea.
Ages 4-7, Grade levels K-2
ISBN: 0671734091

When Nightingale Sings, Thomas, J.
Grade levels 6-9
ISBN: 0060202955

Which Way Is Freedom?, Hensen, Joyce
Obi escapes from slavery during the Civil War, joins a Black Union regiment, and soon becomes involved in the bloody fighting at Fort Pillow, Tennessee. This story illustrates the contributions made by many black soldiers during this conflict.
Grade levels 6-7
ISBN: 0802766366

A White Romance, Hamilton, Virginia
Grade levels 10-12
ISBN: 0399212132

Who Look at Me, Jordan, June
Poetry explains experiences, feelings, and shared past history of black people and implores readers of all ages and races to discover others to look at and see.

Who's in Rabbit's House?, Aardema, Verna
A Masai tale acted out by villagers.
Ages 4-7, Grade levels K-2
ISBN: 0-8037-9549-1

Whose Side Are You ON?, Moore, E.
A sixth grader fails math and is horrified to find out that her new tutor is an old rival. When he disappears, she sets out to find him.
Ages 9- 3, Grade levels 4-7
ISBN: 0374384096

Why the Sun & Moon Live in the Sky, Dayrell
ISBN: 0395539633

Wild Wild Sunflower Child, Pinkney, Jerry
In beautiful verse accompanied by lovely illustrations, Anna revels in the joys of sun, sky, grass, flowers, berries, frogs, and berries.

Wiley and the Hairy Man, Sierra, Judy
An African American folktale about a Bayou boy and how he outsmarted "the Hairy Man" who attempted to carry him away.
Ages 6-9, Grade levels 1-4
ISBN: 0525674772

Will There Be a Lap for Me? Corey, D.
While Kyle's mother is pregnant, he misses not being able to sit on her lap and wonders if after the baby is born will there still be room for him on her lap.
ISBN: 0-8075-9109-2

William and the Good Old Days, Greenfield, Eloise
Ages 3-8, Grade levels Pre-K-3
ISBN: 0060210931

Williamsburg Household, Anderson, Joan
Focuses on events in the household of a Shite family and its enslaved Africans in Colonial Williamsburg in the eighteenth century.
ISBN: 0-89919-516-4; 0-395-54791-1

Willie Bea & the Time the Martians Landed, Hamilton, Virginia
It was Halloween, 1938, and Willie Bea has an experience he'll never forget as his family is caught up in the fear created by Orson Wells "Martians Have Landed" broadcast.
Ages 9-12, Grade levels 4-7
ISBN: 0-689-71328-2

Willy King, Helen Hayes
Nameless ten-year-old feels responsible for capturing a rat (Willy) who has ravaged the family's food supply.

Willie Pearl, Green, Michelle Y.

Willie's Not the Hugging Kind, Barrett, Joyce
Willie's best friend thinks hugging is silly, so Willie makes his family stop hugging him. He soon finds out that he is the hugging kind!
Ages 5-8, Grade levels K-3
ISBN: 0060204176

Willy's Summer Dream, Brown, Kay
Fourteen-year-old Willy, slow in school and ridiculed by other boys, faces another dull summer with his mother until tutoring from a girl and other special experiences help develop a sense of self-confidence.
Ages 12-15, Grade levels 7-10
ISBN: 0152006451

Window Wishing, Craines, Jeannette
Window wishing is window shopping and two black children enjoy this delightful activity when they visit their lively Grandma during vacation.
Ages 5-7, Grade levels 6-7
ISBN: 0-06-020934-8

Winnie Mandela, Neltzer, M.

A Wonderful Terrible Time, Stolz, Mary
Ages 10-11, Grade levels 5-6

Won't Know Till I Get There, Myers, Walter Dean
When Steve tries to impress his new foster brother by painting a name on the side of a subway car, her is caught and their gang must serve time working in an old-age home.
Ages 10-11, Grade levels 5-6
ISBN: 0-14-032612-X

Words By Heart, Sebestyen, Ouida
Ages 4-7, Grade levels K-2
ISBN: 0-316-77931-8

Working Cotton, Williams, Shirley Anne
Young Shelan tells the story of working with her migrant family in the fields of Central California.
Ages 6-7, Grade levels 1-3
ISBN: 0152996249

Yellow Bird and Me, Hansen, Joyce
Through tutoring the class clown, a young girl learns a book can not be judged by its cover.
Ages 12-up, Grade levels 7-up
ISBN: 0-395-55388-1

Your Hand in Mine, Comish, Sam
A small Black boy is lonely and writes verses about things around him. He fends for himself because both of his parents work, but when he forgets his lunch, he realizes that his teacher is his friend.
Ages 8-9, Grade levels 3-4

You're My Nikki, Eisenberg, Phyllis
Nikki fears that her mom will forget about her once she begins a new job.
Grade levels Pre-K-3
ISBN: 0803711298

Young Landlords, Myers, Walter Dean
A gang acquires, by chance, a slum building and a member tells of the gang's efforts to improve the property and to put it on a sound financial basis.
ISBN: 0-14-034244-3

Zeely, Hamilton, Virginia
Two children watch as six-and-a-half-foot tall Zeely glides by day after day, making up romanticized versions of who she is and what her life is like until they meet her and realize who she really is.
Ages 10-13, Grade levels 5-8
ISBN: 0-02-742470-7

Zekmet, **The Stone Carver**, Stolz, Mary
A Tale of Ancient Egypt.
ISBN: 0152999612

Zomo, the Rabbit,
Zomo the rabbit, an African trickster, sets out to gain wisdom.
ISBN: 0152999671

Also available are the Chelsea House Biographical Series on famous African Americans.

The prices range from $7.95 to $18.95.

JUNIOR WORLD BIOGRAPHIES

The subject of these biographies range across history and every field of endeavor, with an emphasis on people whose stories have not often been presented to junior readers, ages 7-12 years old. All titles are hardcover, $13.95/cost, and run approximately 70-72 pages.

TITLES

Matthew Henson	Jesse Owens	Phyllis Wheatley
Nelson Mandela	Harriet Tubman	

BLACK AMERICANS OF ACHIEVEMENTS

Tells the stories of black men and women who have helped shape the course of American history. Written in a straightforward, colorful style for readers of all ages, the series is richly illustrated with photographs, and documents. Each volume contains a bibliography and complete chronology of the subject's life. These books are designed for ages 10 years and older.

In addition, coloring books, puzzles, and paper dolls are also available with African and African-American themes.

TITLES

Muhammad Ali	Richard Allen	Malcolm X
Arthur Ashe	Josephine Baker	James Baldwin
count Basie	Benjamin Banning	James Becks
Mary Mcleod Bethune	George Washington Carver	Charles W. Chestnutt
Bill Cosby	Paul Cuffe	Frederick Douglass
Charles Drew	W.E.B. DuBois	Duke Ellington
Dunbar	Katherine Dunham	Marcus Garvey
James Farmer	Ella Fitzgerald	Matthew Henson
Dizzy Gillespie	Prince Hall	Lena Horne
Chester Hines	Billie Holiday	Jesse Jackson
Langston Hughes	Zora Neale Hurston	Scott Joplin
Jack Johnson	James Weldon	Paul Laurence
Barbara Jordan	Martin Luther King, Jr.	Joe Lewis
Thurgood Marshall	Ronald McNair	Elijah Muhammad
Jesse Owens	Adam Clayton Powell, Jr.	Paul Robeson
Jackie Robinson	Bill Russell	John Ruswurm
A. Phillip Randolph	Harriet Tubman	Nat Turner
Sojourner Truth	Denmark Vessey	Alice Walker
Booker T. Washington	Walter White	Richard Wright

NEW BIOGRAPHIES

New Biographies can be used through many grade levels for reports!

TITLES

Hank Aaron	Count Basie	Charles Chestnutt
Father Devine	Mahalia Jackson	Wilma Rudolph
	Phyllis Wheatley	

LANGUAGE DEVELOPMENT PROGRAM FOR
AFRICAN AMERICAN STUDENTS

African American Children's Literature

Title	Author

PICTURE BOOKS (PRESCHOOL - KND)

Title	Author
A is for Africa	Carey, Jean
Baby Says	Steptoe, John
Big Mama's	Crews, Lucille
Black Mother Goose	Oliver, E.
Brother to the Wind	Walter, Mildred Pitts
Brown Eyes, Brown Skin	Hudson, Cheryl
Calypso Alphabet	Agard, John
Caribbean Alphabet	Lessac, Frane
Caribbean Canvas	Lessac, Frane
Carry, Go, Bring, Come	Samuels, Vyanne
Cherries and Cherries Pits	Williams, Vera B.
Daddy	Gaines, Jeannette
Daddy and I	Greenfield, Eloise
Daniel's Dog	Bogart, JoEllen
Darkness and the Butterfly	Grifalconi, Ann
Daydreamers	Greenfield, Eloise
Doctor Shawn	Breinburg, Petronella
Evan's Corner	Starr Hill, Elizabeth
Everett Anderson's Christmas Coming	Clifton, Lucille
Everett Anderson's Goodbye	Clifton, Lucille
Everett Anderson's Nine Months	Clifton, Lucille
Everett Anderson's Year	Clifton, Lucille
First Pink Light	Greenfield, Eloise
Follow the Drinking Gourd	Winter, Jeanette
Freight Train	Crews, Donald
Galimoto	Williams, Karen
Golden Bear	Young, R.
Good Morning, Baby	Hudson, C. and Wesley, V.
Good Night, Baby	Hudson, C. and Wesley, V.
Grandma's Joy	Greenfield, Eloise

Title	Author
Grandpa's Face	Greenfield, Eloise
I Make Music	Greenfield, Eloise
I Need a Lunchbox	Caines, Jeannette
Island Baby	Keller, Holly
Jamaica and Brianna	Havill, Juanita
Jamaica Tag Along	Havill, Juanita
Jamaica Find	Havill, Juanita
Jamal's Busy Day	Hudson, W.
Josephine's Imagination	Dobrin, Arnold
Joshua's Masai Mask	Hru, D.
My First Kwanzaa	Greenfield, Eloise
Night on Neighborhood Street	Greenfield, Eloise
Not So Fast Songololo	Daily, Niki
One of Three	Johnson, Angela
Osa's Pride	Grifalconi, Ann
Say It Again	Aagard, John
School Bus	Crews, Donald
Shake It to the One You Love the Best	Maddox, C.
Shawn Goes to School	Breinburg, Petronella
Shawn's Red Bike	Breinburg, Petronella
She Come Bringing Me That Little Baby Girl	Greenfield, Eloise
Story of the Jumping Mouse	Steptoe, John
Tell Me a Story Mama	Johnson, Angela
Ten Black Dots	Crews, Donald
Ten, Nine, Eight	Bang, Molly
Truck	Crews, Donald
Ty's One-Man Band	Walter, Mildred Pitts

PRIMARY GRADES   (1ST - 3RD)

Abby	Caines, Jeannette
African Dream	Greenfield, Eloise
Afro-bets Book of Black Heroes From A-Z	Hudson, W. & Wesley, V.
African American Art for Young People	Lewis, Samella
Aida	Price, Leontyne
All Us Come Cross the Water	Clifton, Lucille
Amazing Grace	Hoffman, Mary
Amifika	Clifton, Lucille
A Million Fish...More or Less	McKissack, Patricia

Title	Author
Anansi the Spider	McDermott, Gerald
Anansi the Spider Man	Sherlock, Sir Philip
A Promise to the Sun	Mollet, T.
A Story, a Story	Haley, E.
Aunt Flossie's Hats (and Crab Cakes Later)	Howard, Elizabeth
Back Home	Pinkney, Gloria
Beat the Story Drum, Pum-Pum	Bryan, Ashley
The Boy Who Didn't Believe in Spring	Clifton, Lucille
Boss Cat	Hunter, Kristin
Brown Angels	Myers, Walter Dean
Brown Honey in Broomwheat Tea	Thomas, Joyce
Brown is a Beautiful Color	Bond, Jean Carey
Children of Long Ago	Little, Lessie Jones
Cornrows	Yarbrough, Camille
Count Your Way Through Africa	Haskins, Jim
Do Like Kyla	Johnson, Angela
Don't You Remember	Clifton, Lucille
The Drinking Gourd	Monjo, F. M.
Ears and Tails and Common Sense	Davis, Ossie
Flossie and the Fox	McKissack, Patricia
George Washington Carver	Green, Carol
Good News: Formerly "Buddies"	Greenfield, Eloise
Growin'	Grimes, Nikki
Habari Gani? What's the News A Kwanzaa Story	Morninghouse, Sundaira
Harriet Tubman	Petry, Ann
Honey, I Love	Greenfield, Eloise
Iguana's Tail	Sherlock, Sir Philip
Imani's Gift at Kwanzaa	Patmon, Denise Burden
I Want to Be	Moss, Tylias
Jambo Means Hello	Feelings, Muriel and Tom
Jimmy Lee Did It	Cummings, Pat
Julian's Glorious Summer	Cameron, Ann
Just Us Women	Caines, Jeannette
Kimako's Story	Jordan, June
Kinda Blue	Grifalconi, Ann
Knee-High Man and Other Tales	Lester, Julius
Kwanzaa	Porter, A. P.
Lillie of Watts	Walter, Mildred Pitts
Lil' Sis and Uncle Willie	Everett, Gwen
Make a Joyful Sound	Siler, Deborah (ed.)

Title	Author
Me and Neesie	Greenfield, Eloise
Mirandy and Brother Wind	McKissack, Patricia
Mufaro's Beautiful Daughters (Big book available)	Steptoe, John
Moja Means One	Feelings, Muriel and Tom
More Stories Julian Tells	Cameron, Ann
My Brother Fine with Me	Clifton, Lucille
My Friend Jacob	Clifton, Lucille
My Special Best Words	Steptoe, John
Naja the Snake and Mangus the Mongoose	Kirkpatrick, Oliver
Nathaniel Talking	Greenfield, Eloise
Neesie Jo's Friends	McKissack, Patricia
Oh Kojo, How Could You?	Verna, Aardema
One Smiling Grandma	Linden, A.
Pass It On: African American Poetry for Children	Hudson, W.
Patchwork Quilt	Flournoy, Valeria
Paul Robeson	Greenfield, Eloise
The Picture Book of Martin Luther King, Jr.	Young, Margaret
Picture Life of Malcolm X	Haskins, James
Princess Gorilla and a New Kind of Water	Aardema, Verna
Princess of the Full Moon	Guirma, Frederic
Rabbit Makes a Monkey Out of Lion	Pinkney, Jerry
Rosa Parks	Greenfield, Eloise
Rose for Abby	Guthrie, Donna
Sam Patch, the High, Wide, and Handsome Jumper	Bontemps, Arna
Seven Candles for Kwanzaa	Pinkney, Andrea and Brian
She Wanted to Read	Greenfield, Eloise
Sing to the Sun	Ashley, Bryan
Singing Tales of Africa	Robinson, Adiji
Sidewalk Story	Mathis, Sharon Bell
Some of the Days of Everett Anderson	Clifton, Lucille
Something on My Mind	Grimes, Nikki
Something to Count on	Moore, E.
Songs and Stories from Uganda	Serwadda, William
Soul Looks Back in Wonder	Angelou, Maya et al.
Spin a Soft Black Song	Giovanni, Nikki
Starting Home: The Story of Horace Pippin, Painter	Lyons, Mary
Stevie	Steptoe, John

Title	Author
Stories Julian Tells	Cameron, Ann
Storm in the Night	Stolz, Mary
Sundiata: Lion King of Mali	Wisniewski, David
The Sunflower Garden	Udry, May Janice
Sweet Clara and the Freedom Quilt	Hopkinson, Deborah
Take a Walk in Their Shoes	Turner, Glennette Tiley
Tales of Mogho	Guirma, Frederic
The Tale of Uncle Remus	Lester, Julius
Talk About Family	Greenfield, Eloise
Talking Eggs	San Souci, Robert D.
Tar Beach	Ringgold, Faith
Things I Like About Grandma	Haskin, Francine
The Third Gift	Carew, Jan
Three Wishes	Clifton, Lucille
Tommy Traveler in the World of Black History	Feelings, Tom
Tower of Heaven	Dee, Ruby
Train to Lulu's	Howard, Elizabeth
Train Ride	Steptoe, John
Travelling to Kondo	Aardema, Verna
Turtle Knows Your Name	Ashley, Bryan
The Twins Strike Back	Flournoy, Valerie
Two and Too Much	Walter, Mildred Pitts
Two Ways to Count to Ten	Dee, Ruby
Uncle Jed's Barbershop	Mitchell, M.
Under the Sunday Tree	Greenfield, Eloise
Village of Round and Square Houses	Grifalconi, Ann
Vingananee and the Tree Toad	Aardema, Verna
Walk Together Children	Brown, Ashley
Wave in Her Pocket	Lynn, Joseph
A Weed is a Flower	Aliki
We Keep a Store	Shelby, Anne
We Read: A to Z	Crews, Donald
West Indian Folk Tales	Sherlock, Sir Philip
What Kind of Babysitter is This?	Johnson, D.
What Mary Jo Shared	Udry, Janice May
What's So Funny, Ketu?	Aardema, Verna
When I Am Old With You	Johnson, Angela
When the Rattlesnake Sounds	Childress, Alice
Where Does the Trail Lead?	Burton, Albert
Who Look at Me	Jordan, June

Title	Author
Who's in Rabbit's House	Aardema, Verna
Why Mosquitoes Buzz in People's Ears	Aardema, Verna
Why the Sun and the Moon Live in the Sky	Dayrell
Wiley and the Hairy Man	Bang, Molly
Willie's Not the Hugging Kind	Barrett, Joyce
Window Wishing	Caines, Jeannette
Words By Heart	Sebestyen, Quida
Working Cotton	Williams, Shirley Anne
Your Hand in Mine	Comish, Sam
Zomo, the Rabbit	McDermott, Gerald

UPPER GRADES (4TH - 5TH)

Title	Author
Adventures of High John, The Conqueror	Sanfield, S.
Africa: Brothers and Sisters	Hamilton, Virginia
African American Achievers Series (Doctors, Inventors, Scientists)	
Amos Fortune: Free Man	Yates, Elizabeth
Anthony Burns: The Defeat and Triumph of a Fugitive Slave	Hamilton, Virginia
Arilla Sun Down	Hamilton, Virginia
Ashanti to Zulu	Musgrove, Margaret
Aunt Harriet and the Underground Railroad in the Sky	Ringgold, Faith
Benjamin Banneker	Patterson, Lillie
Black Heroes of the American Revolution	Davis, Burk
Booker T. Washington	Patterson, Lillie
Brother Rush	Hamilton, Virginia
Buffalo Soldiers	Heuman, William
Celebrating Kwanzaa	Hoyt-Goldsmith, Diane
Charlie Parker Played Be Bop	Roshchka, C.
Children of Promise	Sullivan, C.
Childtimes	Greenfield, Eloise
Cousins	Hamilton, Virginia
Dark-Thirty: Southern Tales of the Supernatural	McKissack, Patricia
The Dark Way	Hamilton, Virginia
The Disappearance	Guy, Rosa
Drylongso	Hamilton, Virginia
Dustland	Hamilton, Virginia
Fallen Angels	Myers, Walter Dean
Famous American Negroes	Hughes, Langston
Famous Negro Music Makers	Hughes, Langston

Title	Author
Fannie Lou Hamer	Jordan, June
Frederick Douglass	Bontemps, Arna
The Friendship	Taylor, Mildred
The Gathering	Hamilton, Virginia
Gift-Giver	Hensen, Joyce
The Gold Cadillac	Taylor, Mildred
Have a Happy	Walter, Mildred Pitts
House of Dies Dread	Hamilton, Virginia
Hundred Penny Box	Mathis, Sharon Bell
Ida B. Wells-Barnett: Woman of Courage	Van Steenwyk, Elizabeth
In the Beginning	Hamilton, Virginia
It Ain't All for Nothing	Myers, Walter Dean
Jahdu	Hamilton, Virginia
James Van Der Zee:	
The Picture Takin' Man	Haskins, James
James Weldon Johnson	McKissack, Patricia
Jesse Jackson: A Biography	McKissack, Patricia
Jump at the Sun	Porter, A. P.
Junius Over Far	Hamilton, Virginia
Just Like Martin	Davis, Ossie
Just My Luck	Moore, E.
Justice and Her Brothers	Hamilton, Virginia
Justin and the Best Biscuits in the World	Walter, Mildred Pitts
Koya Delaney and the Good Girls Blues	Greenfield, Eloise
Let the Circle Be Unbroken	Taylor, Mildred
Little Love	Hamilton, Virginia
Long Journey Home	Lester, Julius
Lucky Stone	Clifton, Lucille
The Lost Zoo	Cullen, Countee
Malcolm X: By Any Means Necessary	Myers, Walter Dean
Mariah Keep Cool	Walter, Mildred Pitts
Mariah Loves Rock	Walter, Mildred Pitts
Martin Luther King: A Man to Remember	McKissack, Patricia
Mary McLeod Bethune	Greenfield, Eloise
Me, Mop and the Moondance Kid	Myers, Walter Dean
M. C. Higgins The Great	Hamilton, Virginia
Mississippi Challenge	Walter, Mildred Pitts
My Soul's High Song	Cullen, Countee
Mystery of Dream House	Hamilton, Virginia
Native Artists of Africa	Moore, Reavis

Title	Author
Nat Turner	Griffin, Judith
Nelson Mandela	McKissack, Patricia
Now is Your Time	Myers, Walter Dean
Paul Lawrence Dunbar	McKissack, Patricia
People Could Fly	Hamilton, Virginia
Planet of Junior Brown	Hamilton, Virginia
Reflections of a Black Cowboy	Miller, Robert
Road to Memphis	Taylor, Mildred D.
Roll of Thunder, Hear My Cry	Taylor, Mildred D.
Royal Kingdoms of Ghana: Mali and Songhay	McKissack, Patricia
Scorpions	Myers, Walter Dean
Shimmershine Queens	Yarbrough, Camille
Sister	Greenfield, Eloise
Sojourner Truth: Slave, Abolitionist	Lindstrom, Aletha
Song of The Trees	Taylor, Mildred D.
South Town	Graham, Lorenza
Sticks and Stones, Bobbie Bones	Roberts, Brenda
They Showed the Way	Rollins, Charlemae
Won't Know Till I Get There	Myers, Walter Dean
Yellow Bird and Me	Hansen, Joyce
Young Landlords	Myers, Walter Dean
Zeely	Hamilton, Virginia

AFRICAN AMERICAN LITERATURE FOR CONTRASTIVE ANALYSIS

The following books can facilitate the use of the contrastive analysis strategy suggested for helping African American students understand the differences and similarities between African American Language (AAL) and Mainstream American English (MAE).

Grade	Title	Author
Pre-K-K	She Come Bringing Me That Little Baby Girl	Greenfield, Eloise
K - 1	Flossie and the Fox	McKissack, Patricia
K - 1	Kinda Blue	Grifalconi, Ann
K - 1	Talking Eggs	San Souci, Robert
K - 1	My Brother Fine with Me	Clifton, Lucille
K - 1	People Who Could Fly	Hamilton, Virginia
K - 4	Barber's Cutting Edge	Battle-Levert, G.
1 - 2	The Drinking Gourd	Monjo, F. M.
1 - 7	Sweet Clara and the	
2 - 7	Freedom Quilt	Hopkinson, Deborah
2 - 3	Flossie And The Fox	McKissack, Patricia
2 - 3	Kinda Blue	Grifalconi, Ann
2 - 3	Talking Eggs	San Souci, Robert
2 - 3	People Who Could Fly	Hamilton, Virginia
2 - 3	Double Dutch and Voodoo Shoes	Warren Coleman
4 - 5	The Dragon Takes a Wife	Meyers, Walter Dean
4 - 5	All Us Come Cross the Water	Clifton, Lucille
4 - 5	People Who Could Fly	Hamilton, Virginia
4 - 7	Hundred Penny Box	Mathis, Sharon Bell
5 - 10	Roll of Thunder	Taylor, Mildred D.
5 - 6	Phillip Hall Likes Me, I Reckon	Green, Bette
5 - 9	Patchwork Quilt	Flournoy, Valerie
5 - 8	Shimmershine Queens	Yarbrough, Camille
5 - 9	I Live in Music	Ntozake, Shange
5 - 9	Poetry	Langston Hughes Reader
7 - 10	Mississippi Bridge	Taylor, Mildred D.
7 - 10	Poetry By	Paul Laurence Dunbar

The following books are suitable African and African American Literature to use with students in your classroom. Where we have used a book in Los Angeles, we've included a summary of that book for your information. Additional books are also listed.

A Million Fish . . . More or Less.
McKissack, Patricia
An African American boy begins to suspect that the tall tales about Bayou Clapateaux may be true when he experiences magic. Illustrated by Dena Schutzer in oils in an impressionistic style. Useful for story-telling, for learning about folklore and for reinforcing math concepts.

A Promise to the Sun. Mollel, Tololwa

A Wave in Her Pocket. Joseph, Lynn

Afro-Bets Book of Black Heroes from A to Z. Hudson, Wade
This volume in the Afro-Bets series uses the alphabet as a framework for organizing forty-nine thumbnail sketches of African American and African heroes, living and deceased. A black-and-white photograph (with the exception of one drawing) accompanies each sketch and the biographee's name and main accomplishment are set off by red type. At the bottom of each page, the biographee's name is written again in letters formed by child acrobats. The information is superficial but the book is useful for African American studies.

Ajeemah and His Son. Berry James

The All Jahdu Story Book.
Hamilton, Virginia Zeely
A collection of original folk-like tales about Jahdu, the trickster, by this master storyteller, illustrated with stunning watercolors by Barry Moser. The stories have a mythical quality and use the story form to explain natural phenomena or even colloquial expressions. Useful in studies of African American literature, fantasy, and mythology.

All Night, All Day-A Child's First Book of African American Spirituals. Bryan Ashley
A collection of twenty African American spirituals that have come from the time of slavery and express the realities and hopes of their creators. The musical notation for the voice is supported by piano accompaniments and guitar chords. Illustrated with bright, double-page illustrations. Useful in multicultural and interdisciplinary studies.

Alvin Ailey. Pinkney, Andrea
This biography of African American choreographer Alvin Ailey focuses on his formative years until 1960, when he premiered his modern dance masterpiece, Revelations. Through his determination and motivation, he was able to combine his love of music and his dancing ability to create the Alvin Ailey American Dance Theater, the purpose of which is to explore the Black experience. Expressive, full-page, color scratchboard paintings by Brian Pinkney. Useful in cross-disciplinary studies.

An Island Christmas. Joseph, Lynn

At the Crossroads. Isadora, Rachel
The long-awaited return home of their fathers to their segregated township in South Africa from the mines far away brings a group of children to the crossroads. Their all-night vigil is vividly portrayed in bright, expressive watercolors. A poignant reminder of recent conditions in that country and of the resilience that love brings to family relationships.

Benjie. Lexau, Joan M.

Birthday. Steptoe, John
Javaka Shatu celebrates his eighth birthday in the farming community of Yoruba.

Black Dance in America. Haskin, James
An exciting vibrant history of African American dance in America peppered with full-page, black-and-white pictures. Contains a bibliography, annotated video-graphy, and index. Contains biographical selections as well as general history. Useful in implementing multicultural aspects of curriculum.

Black History for Beginners.
Dennis, Denise
Part of the Writers and Readers Documentary Comic Books series, this book interweaves drawings, photographs, and hand-lettered text in an appealing visual format to introduce readers to African American history from pre-Colonial times to the 1980s. Engaging, with a bibliography but no index. A very useful book for content-based ELL and for reluctant readers to learn about this aspect of American history.

Black Theater in America. Haskins, James
Describes the problems of the African American performers as they struggle toward artistic freedom, cope with discrimination, segregation, and stereotypes. Writing is clear and easily accessible. Includes black-and-white illustrations, bibliography, and index. Useful in gaining understanding of the difficulties of African American performers in finding success.

Booker T. Washington. Patterson, Lillie

Breadsticks and Blessing Places.
Boyd, Candy

Brer Rabbit and the Wonderful Tar Baby.
Metaxas, Eric
Brer Fox tries to get the best of the sassy Brer Rabbit by stirring up a sticky Tar Baby he can run into. Narrated by Danny Glover.

Brown is a Beautiful Color.
Bond, Jean Carvey

Sweet Whispers, Brother Rush.
Hamilton, Virginia
Award: Newbery Honor, 1983
Fourteen-year-old Tree is resentful of, yet loves, her working mother, who is generally absent from the home and who has left Tree in charge of her mentally disabled brother. Through encounters with the ghost of her dead uncle, Tree gains a deeper understanding of her family's problems. This powerful story of poverty, child abuse, and love is told in African American Language and sentence fragments. Useful for African American studies and discussing the above topics.

Can't Sit Still. Lotz, K

Caribbean Alphabet. Lessac, Frane

Caribbean Canvas. Lessac, Frane
A collection of art reproductions of paintings by
Caribbean primitive-styles artist, Frane Lessac,
combined with poems written in the vernacular
of island speech. Large attractive format. The
unfamiliar use of language will need explanation.
A joyous celebration of island life, art, and
poetry. Useful in diversity education.

Carousel. Cruz, Donald

Cat in the Mirror. Stolz, Mary

Chilly Stomach. Caines, Jeannette
A look at the confusion and uncertainty resulting
from unwanted touching. Three different
scenarios present clear differences.

Circle of Gold. Boyd, Candy
After Mattie's father dies, her mother can't seem
to cope with day-to-day responsibilities. Mattie
feels rejected and devises a plan to win back her
mother's love. Sympathetic African American
characters. Useful in discussion on honesty,
family relationships, Mother's Day, gifts, and
independence.

Crocodile and Hen. Lexau, Joan M

Dancing with the Indians. Medearis, Angela
Based on a true incident described in an

afterword, *Dancing With The Indians* depicts
Native Americans and African Americans
dancing together at a Seminole pow-wow. The
rhyme pattern is less than perfect, but the
narrative abounds with imagery. Illustrations
glowing with light fill the pages. A good read-
aloud for multicultural studies.

The Dark Way. Hamilton, Virginia

(The) Day They Stole the Letter "J".

The Dear One. Woodson, Jacqueline
When pregnant, fifteen-year-old Rebecca comes
to live with thirteen-year-old Feni in suburban
Seton, Pennsylvania. Both girls have to
overcome stereotypical opinions about each
other's lifestyle and families before they can
accept each other as they are. Depicts
successful, assertive, African American women
as positive role models. Well-defined characters
make this novel useful in units on family life,
maturation, and modern lifestyles.

Definitely Cool. Wilkinson, Brenda
Headed for her first day at Riverdale Junior High,
a new school in a fancy new neighborhood,
twelve-year-old African American Roxanne tries
to figure out how to make friends while staying
cool. Good dialogue and slang, realistic action,
and believable characters combine to create a
refreshing look at modern adolescence. Great
cover and short chapters will maintain interest.
Useful in units on peer relationships, maturation,
and adjusting to change.

Dinner at Aunt Connie's House.
Ringgold, Faith
Melody and her cousin, Lonnie, learn about
courageous and talented women in African

American history when Aunt Connie's paintings speak to them. Based upon a quilt with the same title by the artist that combines painting, sewing, and storytelling. Appealing and colorful, the book is useful in the study of women, African American history, heroes and heroines, and art.

The Disappearance. Guy, R.

Down in the Piney Woods. Smothers, Ethel
Through a series of vignettes, the author portrays a strong African American sharecropper family in rural Georgia in the 1950s. When ten-year-old Annie Rye's stepsisters move into the house, she not only experiences anger with them and her family, but encounters prejudice and hatred from the community. Creates a vivid sense of place and character. Useful for discussing the African American experience.

Duke Ellington. Collier, James
This engrossing biography includes an examination of Ellington's music as well as a description of his personal life and the social conditions of his times. Fascinating details of his methods of composing, of organizing his band and the abilities and styles of the musicians with whom he worked are described in a lively style. Includes suggestions for further study and an index. Useful for the music curriculum and for African American studies.

Emily and the Klunky Baby and **The Next-Door Dog**. Lexau, Joan M.

Fashion By Tasha.   Johnson, S.

Femi and Old Grandaddie.   Robinson, Adjai

Ferris Wheel.   Stolz, Mary

For the Life of Leatitia.   Hodge, M.

Forever Friends.   Boyd, Candy
Twelve-year-old Toni Douglas is having a difficult time mastering sixth-grade math, adjusting to her maturation, and getting her two friends Mattie and Susan to like one another. When Susan is tragically killed in an automobile accident, it is Mattie that helps her adjust to the death. Contains much mathematical imagery surrounding a loving African American family. Useful for discussing mathematics in our world, maturation, death, and friendship.

Freedom Songs. Moore, Yvette
A trip down South in the 1960s from her comfortable, all-black, Brooklyn neighborhood opens fourteen-year-old Sheryl's eyes to the injustices endured by African Americans there. When her beloved Uncle Pete joins the freedom riders, she helps to organize a gospel concert up North to defray the group's expenses. Though the characters have good intentions, dramatic tension is lacking. Useful in the study of Civil Rights in African American studies.

The Friends. Guy, R.

From Miss Ida's Porch. Belton, Sandra
An African American girl describes the best time of day hearing old folks tell stories on Miss Ida's porch, especially the stories about when Duke Ellington and Marion Anderson came to town. Soft, expressive pastels by Floyd Cooper add a sense of beauty and warmth to this close neighborhood scene. Useful for discussing music, civil rights, memories, and African American history.

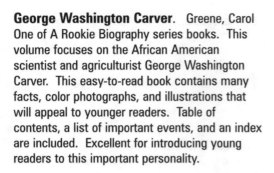

George Washington Carver. Greene, Carol
One of A Rookie Biography series books. This
volume focuses on the African American
scientist and agriculturist George Washington
Carver. This easy-to-read book contains many
facts, color photographs, and illustrations that
will appeal to younger readers. Table of
contents, a list of important events, and an index
are included. Excellent for introducing young
readers to this important personality.

The Girl Who Worse Snakes.
Johnson, Angela

Golden Bear.   Young, Ruth
An African American child and his special
playmate, a golden bear, enjoy a warm bond of
friendship in this story told in rhyme and song.
The brilliantly colored, full-page paintings
celebrate their relationship. Useful for initiating
discussions about imaginary playmates and
friendship and a good bedtime story.

Going Swimming.   Berridge, Celia

The Gold Cadillac.   Taylor, Mildred D.
Told through the eyes of a young girl, this
historical fiction story is of an African American
family from Ohio in the 1950s. The father buys
a gold Cadillac against the mother's wishes.
Despite warnings, they drive the car South to
Mississippi to visit relatives, experiencing
first hand the ignorance and prejudice there.
Powerfully and sensitively written. Depicts
strong family relationships. Sepia illustrations
enhance the text. Useful in discussing diversity,
prejudice, and race relations.

The Great Migration.   Lawrence, Jacob
Around the time of World War I, large numbers

of African American people moved North in
search for a better life. African American artist
Jacob Lawrence chronicled this migration in
sixty paintings, some of which make up the
illustrations in this book. Accompanied by a
lyrical text, this book is useful in the study of art
appreciation, African American artists,
migrations, and World War I.

The Great Rebellion.   Stolz, Mary

The Green Lion of Zion Street.   Fields, Julia
The text, written in verse format in AAL,
describes how a group of children who have
missed their bus on a cold afternoon, take a
walk to visit a huge stone lion that reigns over
Zion Street. The children imagine that he is
alive. Illustrated by Jerry Pinkney in beautiful
watercolor. A read-aloud, useful for discussing
city life, imaginative thinking, and for developing
descriptive language.

Growing.   Grimes, Nikki
Two young African Americans who have
experienced loss, grief, and death become
friends and learn together how to cope with the
maturation process. Easy-to-read text. Useful
for discussion on relationships, growing-up,
school problems such as bullies and
adolescence.

Happy Birthday, Martin Luther King.
Marzollo, Jean
In simple language directed at young children,
the author shares the life, dreams, and
accomplishments of this great Civil Rights
leader. Illustrated by Brian Pinkney using
scratchboard and oil pastels. An excellent book
to use to explain to children why we honor this
African American hero.

Harbor.   Crews, Donald

Harriet and the Promised Land.
Lawrence, Jacob
This is a reissue, with a new introduction by
Jacob Lawrence, of a book about Harriet
Tubman, the slave who led many of her people
North to freedom. Simple rhyming verses tell
her story. Stylized paintings by Lawrence, a
famous African American artist, forcefully depict
the degradation of slavery. Extends the fifth
grade core book *House of Dies Drear*. Useful for
studying about African Americans and slavery
and to read aloud as part of a biography unit.

Hear My Cry.   Taylor, Mildred
Set in Mississippi in 1993, this novel, told from
ten-year-old Cassie Logan's point of view,
focuses on the prejudicial and unequal treatment
of African Americans and the Logan family's
struggle to keep their land. This compelling
historical novel, filled with vivid characters and
AAL, is useful in the study of American history
and African Americans.

How the Leopard Got His Spots.
Glower, D

I Love My Family. Hudson Wade

I am a Jesse White Tumbler.
Schmidt, Diane
Kenyon Connor, an African American eighth-
grader who has been a member of the Chicago-
based Jesse White Tumbling team since age
five, describes the team's shows, routines, and
positive aspects and influences, especially the
importance of discipline, team work, and
commitment. Illustrated with numerous, action-
packed, color photographs. An excellent photo
documentary to use in multicultural and physical
education units.

Sing to the Sun.   Bryan, Ashley
A collection of original poems in celebration of
life. Some reflect a Caribbean setting. Each
page carries an illustration by the author in
vibrant color in a design comparable to the
quality of stained glass. Useful for art
appreciation, multicultural studies, and African
American studies.

Indigo and Moonlight Gold.   Gilchrist, Jan
Autie, a young African American girl,
contemplates the passage of time and the
changes that time brings on one starry, moonlit
night. Lovely oil paintings by Jan Spivey
Gilchrist depict a loving mother/daughter
relationship. A quiet, lyrical story useful for
contemplating change, time, and growing up.

It Ain't All for Nothing. Myers, Walter Dean

Jamal's Busy Day.   Hudson, Wade
Part of the Feeling Good series, a young African
American boy details his busy day during which,
like his architect father and accountant mother,
he works with numbers, attends meetings, and
settles disputes between coworkers. George
Ford's watercolors, while appealing, appear
slightly out of focus. Didactic but useful for
reinforcing the values of hard work, a positive
attitude, and self-esteem. Could be used in
career education.

Jambo Means Hello.   Feelings, M
Swahili Alphabet Book--Examples of African life
depict each of the 24 letters of the Swahili
alphabet.

James Van Der Zee. Haskins, James
Based upon interviews with the late James Van Der zee, this book chronicles the life and work of this respected African American photographer whose life spanned nearly a century and whose pictures are considered classics in their depiction of the Harlem Renaissance. Includes many black-and-white photographs. Excellent in the study of photograph, this era, and biography.

Jesse Jackson. McKissack, Patricia
A biography of African American leader Jesse Jackson that traces his life from his birth in 1941 in South Carolina, to his involvement with Civil Rights, to his bid for the presidency, and up to the present. Illustrated with black-and-white photographs. While acknowledging controversial opinions, the book conveys a favorable attitude. Contains a bibliography and index. Useful in United States history and multicultural studies as well as in biography units.

John Brown. Graham, Lorenz

Jonathan and His Mommy.
Small-Hector, Irene

Joshua's Masai Mask. Hru, Dakari
Joshua, an African American boy, worried that his friends will laugh at him for playing his uncle Zambezi's kalimba at the school talent show, wishes he were cool like Kareem, or Righteous Rapper, or even the mayor. When he magically becomes these others, he learns to value who he is. Attractive acrylic paintings by Ann Rich. Somewhat contrived plot. Useful for thinking about self-esteem and identity.

Jump at De Sun. Porter, A.P.
A well-written biography of African American author and folklorist Zora Neale Hurston that reveals her creativity and dedication to folklore and African American literature as well as her personal foibles and weaknesses. Includes black-and-white photographs and drawings, afterword, notes, an excellent bibliography, and index. An extremely accessible introduction to extend the study of African American authors and literature.

Junius Over Far. Hamilton, Virginia
Fourteen-year-old Junius's mentally deteriorating grandfather returns to his Caribbean island home. As they rescue the grandfather from danger, Junius and his father discover their island heritage, composed of tropical beauty and the legacy of slavery. This is a perceptive and empathetic portrayal of complex characters and relationships as well as the effects of aging. Excellent for studying about senior citizens, African Americans, the complex relationships between master and slave, and the relationships between family members.

Last Summer with Maizon. Woodson, Jacqueline
When best friends Margaret and Maizon are eleven years old, Margaret's father dies and Maizon is accepted to an exclusive boarding school. The friend's last summer together in Broklyn reveals the depth of their friendship, their anxieties and fears about the impending separation, and the strength their families provide them. Useful in units on African Americans and family life.

Let's Be Enemies. Udry, Janice May

Let's Hear It for the Queen.
Childress, Alice

Let's Make Music.

Life and Times of a Free Black Man.
Hamilton, Virginia

Lift Every Voice and Sing.
Johnson, James Weldon
Jan Gilchrist, a Coretta Scott King award-winning artist, presents illustrations for the song by James Weldon Johnson, "Lift Every Voice and Sing," known as the African American national anthem. The musical score is included. Lovely impressionistic artwork in colored pencil, gouache, and watercolors accompanied by calligraphy. A good source for singing and reinforcing pride and self-esteem.

A Little Love. Hamilton, Virginia

Ludell and Willie. Wilkinson, Brenda
The second book of a trilogy, Ludell and Willie are seniors in a Georgia segregated high school in the early 1960s. Raised by her very strict grandmother, Ludell is looking forward to graduation and marriage to Willie. Mama's sudden death brings an abrupt end to their plans when Ludell's biological mother takes her back to New York to live. The AAL is at times quite difficult to follow. Useful for recreational reading and looking at family values.

Mac and Marie & The Train Toss Surprise. Howard, Elizabeth
A brother and sister, Mac and Marie, await the train that runs by their house, anticipating the surprise package their uncle has promised them. An introductory note tells that Mac, the author's father, never was able to realize his dream of becoming a train engineer because he was an

African American living at the turn of the century. Colorful illustrations extend the warmth of the evocative text. Useful for African American studies and units on transportation.

Malcolm X. Adoff, Arnold
A biography of Malcolm X, who suffered much as a child and who at age twenty, was sent to prison for robbery. In prison he had access to a library, which changed his life and projected him into the role of a world leader. Written in clear and direct prose. The author has shown Malcom's strengths as well as his weaknesses. Shortness invites oversimplifications. No source material. Black-and-white illustrations. Useful as an introduction to this African American's life or for units on civil rights, Black Muslims, or prejudice.

Mirandy and Brother Wind.
McKissack, Patricia
Mirandy looks to Brother Wind to help to win the Junior Cakewalk.

Marked by Fire. Thomas, J.

Mary Had a Little Lamb. Hale, Sarah
The nursery rhyme about Mary and her lamb is retold with photographs showing an African American child caring for a real lamb. Includes the history of the rhyme, written by Sarah Hale in 1830, and the original rhyme. A wonderful way to extend the study of folk rhymes and American history.

Messy Bessey's Closet. McKissack, Patricia

Meet Addy. Porter, C.

Millicent's Ghost. Lexau, Joan M

Mojo Means One. Feelings, M
Swahili Counting Book - Each number from one
to ten is illustrated with some aspect of East
African life.

Monkey-Monkey's Trick.
McKissack, Patricia

Moon Jumbers. Udry, Janice May

Mr. Monkey & The Gocha Bush.
Myers, Walter

Mufaro's Beautiful Daughters.
Steptoe, John
African folklore where two daughters-one selfish
and the other very sweet-hope to marry the king
who's searching for a wife.

The Music Maker. Guy, R.

My Little Island. Lessac, Frane
A little boy takes Lucca, his best friend, to visit
his homeland in the Caribbean.

My Special Best Words. Steptoe, John

My Soul Looks Back in Wonder. Feeling, T.

Nelson Mandela. McKissack, Patricia

New Guys Around the Block. Guy, R

Nini at Carnival. Lloyd, Errol

The Noonday Friends.

Not Yet. Ketteman, Helen
Yvette and her father spend the day preparing
for her mother's birthday. The father responds
patiently each time little Yvette asks, "Is it time
yet?" Full-color illustrations successfully portray
the warmth of a close-knit, African American
family. Useful for providing positive, African
American role models in a study of family life.

The Orphan Boy. Mollel, Tololwa
Though delighted that an orphan boy has come
into his life, an old man becomes insatiably
curious about the boy's mysterious powers.

Out from This Place. Hansen, Joyce
In this sequel to *Which Way Freedom?*, fourteen-
year-old Easter, a runaway slave, struggles to
make decisions about her future: should she
stay in the South and marry Julius, should she
continue her search for her beloved Obi, or
should she go to the North and get an
education? This historical novel focuses on the
bitter-sweet taste of freedom. Useful in
understanding the problems faced by African
Americans at the end of the Civil War. In
conjunction with the previous book, it develops
a strong sense of point of view.

Outside Shot. Myers, Walter Dean

The Party. Johnson, S.

The Picture Life of Malcolm X.
Haskins, James

Plain City. Hamilton, Virginia
Twelve-year-old Buhlaire-Marie Sims, a blonde, fair-skinned African American girl, feels like an outsider in Plain City. When she learns that her father, whom she thought had died, is alive, her world changes and she must accept the truth about his mental illness. Written in a clipped, conversational style, woven with an on-going interior monologue. A story about alienation, family secrets, and an adolescent's search for identity and self-esteem.

Poor Girl, Rich Girl. Wilson, Johnniece
When fourteen-year-old African-American Miranda, who wants to get contact lenses, finds that her parents can't afford them, she sets out to get a job and earn the money herself. In the process she tries a variety of jobs, learns to make a friend, and finally begins to like and excel at cooking. Warm family relationships make this a good book for discussing family life, money, and the pros and cons of different jobs.

The Prince. Johnson, S.

Princess Gorilla and a New Kind of Water. Aardema, Verna
King Gorilla decrees that no one may marry his daughter until a suitor strong enough to consume a barrel of strange, smelley water can be found.

Quentin Corn. Stolz, Mary

Say It Again, Granny. Aagard, John

School Bus. Crews, Donald
Shake It to the One That You Love Best.
Mattox, Cheryl
Music and lyrics for African American children's songs. With each song is a notation indicating

the culture most closely associated with the version presented. Instructions are provided for the sixteen game songs and background information is provided for the ten lullabies. Vanette P. Honeywood's striking, stylized collages and Brenda Joysmith's glowing, impressionistic pastels capture the warmth of the culture. Each page is bordered with strips of *kente* cloth. Index included. Useful for appreciation for their culture.

Singing Tales of Africa. Robinson, Adjai
The author retells seven of his favorite tall-tales that are meant to be shared. Musical scores are here along with African lyrics and English translations.

Siri the Conquistador. Stolz, Mary

Sky Man. Johnson, S.

Solomon's Secret. Pirotta, Savior
When Solomon visits his neighbors, Mr. & Mrs. Zee, for afternoon tea, he discovers their background harbors exotic adventures and limitless possibilities.

Something to Count on. Moore, E.

Song and Stories from Uganda.
Serwadda, William
Have fun with this book filled with songs and stories.

Sport Page. Adolph, A.

Sticks and Stones, Bobbie Bones. Roberts
It's tough when Bobbie has to move to a new neighborthoodand attend a new school. It's even tougher when Big Myra decides that she

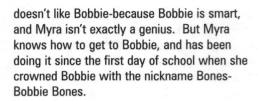

doesn't like Bobbie-because Bobbie is smart, and Myra isn't exactly a genius. But Myra knows how to get to Bobbie, and has been doing it since the first day of school when she crowned Bobbie with the nickname Bones-Bobbie Bones.

Striped Ice Cream. Lexau, Joan M.
Becky, the youngest child in a single-parent African American family, is rejected by her family members as her birthday draws near, only to discover that they have been planning to surprise her with her favorite ice cream dessert and a new dress in the same colors as the dessert. Pastel drawings by John Wilson. A quiet tale focusing on birthdays, family life, loving relationships, and surprises.

The Sunflower Garden. Udry, May Janice

Susannah and the Blue House Mystery. Elmore, P.

Susannah and the Purple Mongoose Mystery. Elmore, P.

T for Tommy. Lexau, Joan M

Tailypo. Wahl, Jan
A retelling of the African American folktale about an old man and a monster that repeatedly moans about wanting back his tail or "tailypo." Gruesome, scary story. Wil Clay's colorful, acrylic paintings add to the suspense. Useful for telling or reading aloud with the lights out.
Themba. Sacks, M.

This Is The Key to the Kingdom.
Allison, Diane
A familiar nursery rhyme is the basis for this picture book. An African American girl travels through a land of make-believe to a kingdom, a city, a town, a street, a lane, etc. When she returns home, she brings back a flower and gives it to a street musician. The imaginary scenes of the nursery rhyme are illustrated with soft and very pale watercolors, while the realistic scenes are more vivid. Can be used to motivate students to create their own imaginary worlds and tell or write about what they would see there.

Three African Tales. Robinson, Adjai

Tickle Tickle.

Tituba of Salem. Petry, A.

Tommy Traveler in the World of Black History.

Toning the Sweep. Johnson, Angela
When fourteen-year-old Emily and her mother go to the California desert to help her grandmother prepare to go back to Cleveland to die, she discovers much about her grandfather's death, family relationships, her feelings about the desert, and comes to a new understanding of her mother. As Emily uses a camcorder to record the life in the desert and the people who love her grandmother, she captures the warmth and love of an African American family. Useful in discussing the above issues.

The Twins Strike Back. Flournoy, Valerie

Uncle Jed's Barbershop.
Mitchell, Margares
Young African American girl raised in the segregated 1920s recalls her favorite relative, her generous great-uncle Jed, and his perseverance in pursuing the dream of one day owning a barbershop. Realistic paintings by James Ransome depict the strength and warmth of the people. Useful for African American studies and to motivate perseverance in pursuit of goals.

Underground Man.   Meltzer, M.

Ups and Downs of Carl Davis III.
Guy, Rosa

W. E. B. DuBois.   Hamilton, Viriginia
A reissue of the carefully researched and documented biography of the late nineteenth and early twentieth century African American civil rights leader and author W. E. B. DuBois. His story is sympathetically, yet candidly, told. Some photographs add to the compelling text. Chapter notes, a bibliography, and an index are included. Use for American history and biography units.

West Indian Folk Tales.   Sherlock, Sir Philip

When the Nightingale Sings.
Thomas Joyce
Fourteen-year-old Marigold is an orphan whose superlative singing talents are being hidden by the mean woman and her two bickering twin daughters with whom she lives. The search for a new lead gospel singer for a famous church choir allows Marigold to perform in a public setting and to learn about her family history. A skillful blending of fairy tale elements, gospel music, and Southern culture into a lyrical, vibrant, African American Cinderella story.

A White Romance.   Hamilton, Virginia
Confronting the invasion of white students into her African American high school, Talley

reluctantly makes friends with a white girl and is drawn into a sexual relationship with a drug-dealing, white boy. Contains AAL and explicit sex. Paints a realistic portrait of an African American teenager stuggling to develop her own sense of values and self-esteem.

Why the Sun & Moon Live in the Sky.
Dayrell

William and the Good Old Days.
Greenfield, Elosie
William, a young African American boy, remembers the good old days visiting his grandmother's restaurant before she got too sick to work. Expressive color illustrations by Jan Spivey Gilchrist. Written in a lyrical style that captures the warmth of community and family and the boy's hope for the future. A good read-aloud for focusing on these issues.

Willy, King.   Hayes, Helen

Willie Pearl.   Green, Michelle

Winnie Mandela.   Neltzer, M.

A Wonderful Terrible Time.   Stolz, Mary

Words by Heart.
Sebestyen, OuidaCore
In 1910, twelve-year-old Lena's African American family moves from the South to the cotten fields of the West where her father, Ben, feels his children will have a better future. Here Lena first encounters prejudice and hate, which leads to her father's murder and her need to take up his crusade to fight hate with love. Beautifully written. Useful in multicultural studies for thinking about diversity and race relations.

RESOURCE LIBRARY AND DATABASE

LOS ANGELES UNIFIED SCHOOL DISTRICT
DIVISION OF INSTRUCTION
Language Acquisition and Bilingual Development Branch

Language Development Program for African American Students

BOOKS AND JOURNALS

RESEARCH ARTICLES AND PERIODICALS

AFRICAN AMERICAN CHILDREN'S LITERATURE

COMPUTER SOFTWARE & VIDEO PROGRAMS

REFERENCE BOOKS AND JOURNALS
CODES AND CATEGORIES

ABBREVIATED CODE	REFERENCE CATEGORY
AAL	AFRICAN AMERICAN LANGUAGE
AAL	AFRICAN AMERICAN LANGUAGE
ALM	AFRICAN LIBERATION MOVEMENT
AAM	AFRICAN AMERICAN MALES
BE	BILINGUAL EDUCATION
C	CULTURE
CT	CRITICAL THINKING
D	DEMOGRAPHICS
DR	DROP-OUT RATE
E	EDUCATION
EAA	EDUCATION & AFRICAN AMERICANS
EM	EDUCATING MINORITIES
H	HISTORY
L	LITERATURE
LA	LANGUAGE ACQUISITION
MAE	MAINSTREAM AMERICAN ENGLISH
ME	MULTICULTURAL EDUCATION
MS	MATH AND SCIENCE
NC	NON-CIRCULATING
P	PARENT RESOURCE
R	REFERENCE
S	SELF-ESTEEM
T	TEACHER RESOURCE
TA	THEMATIC APPROACH
TE	TESTING
W	WHOLE LANGUAGE
WP	WRITING PROCESS

TITLE	AUTHOR	CATEGORY
A Crash Course In Black History: 150 Important Facts About Afrikan Peoples	Kondo, Zak,	H
A Host of Tongues: Language Communities in the United States	Conklin, Nancy	LA
A Talk with Jawanza: Critical Issues in Educating African American Youth	Kunjufu, Jawanza	EAA
Africa in Class Antiquity	Office of Curriculum	H-NC
African American History: Heroes in Hardship	Stevenson, Lisbeth	H
Africanisms in American Culture	Holloway, Joseph E.	C
Africanisms in the Gullah Dialect	Turner, Lorenzo D.	AAL
Afrocentric: Self Inventory	Perkins, Useni	C
Alphablack Culture: Beginning Activity Book	Issac, Mia	C
Bellwork: A Daily Reading and Activity Book Written Language Practice Program Level Three Part 1	Kinney, Margaret	T
Bellwork: A Daily Reading and Written Language Practice Program Level Three Part 2	Kinney, Margaret	T
Black Children: Their Roots, Culture and Learning Styles	Hale Benson, Janice	C
Black English: Educational Equity and the Law	Chamber, John	AAL
Black Scientists of America	Donovan, Richard	H
Black Street Speech: It's History Structure and Survival	Baugh, John	AAL
Black Vernacular and Vocabulary	Fols, Edith	AAL-NC
Black Voices: An Anthology of Afro-American Literature	Chapman, Abraham	C-NC
Blueprint for Success	Business Week	T
Caught in the Middle: How to Unleash the Potential of Average Students	Gonder, Peggy Odell	E
Children's Speech: A Practical Introduction to Communication	Hopper, Robert	L

TITLE	AUTHOR	CATEGORY
Development-Second Edition Class Language & Education	NewSum, H.E	C
Countering the Conspiracy to Destroy Black Boys	Kunjufu, Jawanza	AAM
Countering the Conspiracy to Destroy Black Boys Volume II	Kunjufu, Jawanza	AAM
Cultural Genocide in the Black and African Studies Curriculum	Ben-Jochannan, Yosef	EAA
Decolonising The Mind	Thiong'o, Ngugi Wa	C
Developing Minds	Arthur Costa	CT-NC
Developing Positive Self-Images and Discipline in Black Children	Kunjifi, Jawanza	P
Different and Wonderful	Hopson, Darlene, Ph.D	P
Discourse and Discrimination	Smitherman-Donaldson	C
Empowering Minority Students	Cummins, Jim	EM
Encyclopedia of Black America	Low, W. Augustus, Editor	C-NC
Going for the Gold	Bentley, Ken	H
Handbook For Planning an Effective Writing Program	California State Department	WR
He-Said-She-Said:Talk As Social Orginization Among Black Children	Goodwin, Marjorie HA	AAL
Helping Your Child To Success	Davis, Julia Alford	EEA
I Cry For My Parents	Issac, Mia	P
If You're Trying To Teach Kids How to Write You've Gotta Have This Book!	Frank, Marjorie	T
Instructed Second Language Acquisition	Ellis, Rod	L
Journal of Black Studies-Volume 21, #4 June 1991	Asante, Molefi Editor	C-NC
Journal of Black Studies-Volume 21, #1 September 1990	Asante, Molefi Editor	C-NC
Journal of Black Studies-Volume 21, #2 December 1990	Asante, Molefi Editor	C-NC
Journal of Black Studies-Volume 21, #3 March 1991	Asante, Molefi Editor	C-NC
Language Competence Assessment and Intervention	Schiefelbusch, Richard	L
Lessons from History: A Celebration in Blackness—Elementary Edition	Kunjufu, Jawanza	H

TITLE	AUTHOR	CATEGORY
Multicultural Education in a Pluralistic Society Third Edition	Gollrick, Donna	E
Nature of Communication Disorders in Culturally and Linguistically Diverse Population	Taylor, Orlando, Ph.D	L
Once Upon a TIme When We Were Colored	Taulbert, Clifton	C
Parent Workshop Guide	Livingston, Dr. Nancy	T-NC
Parents as Partners in Reading	Edwards, Patricfia, Ph.D	P-NC
Practical Ideas for Reading and Writing a Process	Olson, Carol Booth, E.d	WR
Recommended Readings in Literature	Language Arts	T
Resources List for Elementary School Library Media Centers 1990-91	Office and Instruction	T-NC
Studies for Immersion Education: A Collection for the United States Educators	Office of Bilingual BIC	E
Talk That Talk an Anthology of African American Storytelling	Goss, Linda, Ed.	AAL
Talkin and Testifying The Language of Black America	Smitherman, Geneva	AAL
Tapping Potential: English and Language Arts for the Black Learner	Brooks, Charlotte, EDI	EAA
Teaching Standard English in the Inner City	Fasold, Ralph	AAL
The African Origin of Civilization: Myth Or Reality	Diop, Cheanta and M.	H
The Afrocentric Idea	Asante, Molefi Kete	C
The Black Manager	Dickens, Floyd, Jr.	R-NC
The Black Poets	Randall, Dudley	C-NC
The Black Students Guide to Positive Education	Kodo, Babazak	EAA
The Creative Curriculum for Early Childhood	Dodge, Diane	T
The Cultural Unity of Black Africa	Diop Cheikh Anta	C
The Development Pyschology of the Black Child	Wilson, Amos	C
The Mis-Education of the Negro	Woodson, Carter G.	EAA
The Whole Language Catalog	Goodman, Kenneth	W

TITLE	AUTHOR	CATEGORY
The Words of Martin Luther King, Jr.	King, Coretta Scott	H
They Came Before Columbus	Sertima, Ivan Van	H
To Be Popular or Smart the Black Peer Group	Kunjufu, Jawanza	EAA
Toward Black Self Esteem	Staff of the California	E
Treatment of Communication Disorders in Culturally and Linguistically Diverse Population	Taylor, Orlanda, Ph.D	L
Twice as Less	Orr, Eleanor Wilson	MS
Verbal Image Enhancement	Cole, Lorianne, Ph.D	AAL-NC
We Are Our Own Educators	Jones, Valentino	EAA
What's Whole in Whole Language	Goodman, Ken	W
Whole Language Sourcebook	Baskwill, June	W-NC
With Different Eyes	Peitzman, Faye	EM-NC

ABBREVIATED CODE	REFERENCE CATEGORY
AAL	AFRICAN AMERICAN LANGUAGE
ALM	AFRICAN LIBERATION MOVEMENT
AAM	AFRICAN AMERICAN MALES
BE	BILINGUAL EDUCATION
C	CULTURE
CT	CRITICAL THINKING
D	DEMOGRAPHICS
DR	DROP-OUT RATE
E	EDUCATION
EAA	EDUCATION & AFRICAN AMERICANS
EM	EDUCATING MINORITIES
H	HISTORY
L	LITERATURE
LA	LANGUAGE ACQUISITION
MAE	MAINSTREAM AMERICAN ENGLISH
MS	MATH AND SCIENCE
NC	NON-CIRCULATING
P	PARENT RESOURCE
R	REFERENCE
T	TEACHER RESOURCE
TA	THEMATIC APPROACH
TE	TESTING
W	WHOLE LANGUAGE

LOS ANGELES UNIFIED SCHOOL DISTRICT

Language Acquisition and Bilingual Development Branch

Language Development Program for African American Students

RESEARCH ARTICLES AND PERIODICALS

TITLE	AUTHOR	DATE	SOURCE	CATEGORY
A (Vague) Sense of History	Alter, Jonathan		Newsweek	H
A Decade of Educational Reform Results in Only Minor Program	National Assessment			EM
A Linguistic Description of Nonstandard English		10/77	Social Dialects	AAL
A Scenario for the Implementation of the "Thinktrix" at the Primary	Koza, Nancy		unknown	CT CG
Africa: Drifting off the Map of the Worlds Concerns	Lone, Salim	8/24/90	Herald Tribune	EAA
African History	Sweeting, Earl	1973	African American II	H
	Viadero, Debra	1/14/90	Educational Week	EAA
Afro-Centric Study Boosts Performance by Black Students				
An Investigation of Transfer Second Language Phonology	Broselow, Ellen			AALCI
An Urban High School in the "Kindergarten Tradition"	Clinchy, Evans		Equity and Choice	
Anthropology and Multicultural Education: Classroom AP	Moses, Yolonda	12/5/81	Paper No. 38	M
Anthropology and Multicultural Education: Classroom APP	Nuri-Robins, Kika	12/5/81	Publication 83-1: ANT	AAC
Baltimore Class Tests Theory of Providing Positive Role Model	Viadero, Debra	2/3/91	Education Week	AAM
Battle Over Multicultural Education	Viadero, Debra		Education Week	M

TITLE	AUTHOR	DATE	SOURCE	CATEGORY
Education Rises in Intensity	Carter, Marlene		Observation Report	AAL
Best of Both Worlds, The	Krashen, Stephen			BE
Bilingual Education and Second Language Acquisition Theory				
Bilingual Education: Language Learning and Politics	Crawford, James	4/1/87	Education Week	BE
Bilingual Education: The Choice The Effectiveness Debate	Crawford, James	1990	Equity and Choice	BE
Black English Dialect and the Classroom Teacher	Alexander, Clara			AAL
Black Teenager in Young Adult Novels by Award Winning Authors	Kiah, Rosalie Bla,			AAC
Calexio Defies Odds on Drop-Out Rate	Hillinger, Charles	6/13/91	Los Angeles Times	DO
California State Board of Public Instruction Policy Statement		4/85		AAL
Classroom Changes Give a Feel for Math, Science	Roark, Annie C.	11/9/90	Los Angeles Times	MS
Cognitive Apprenticeship: Making Thinking Visible	Collins, Allan and B.	Winter 199	American Educators	
Columbus Discovery Rates No Celebration	Bigelow, Bill	10/91	California Teacher	ME
Committee to Study the Status of the Black Male in the Public		86-87	New Orleans Public	AAM
Critical Issues in Educating African American Youth	Kunjufu, Jawanza			EAA
Culture, Schooling and Eurocentrism	Raspberry, Willi		Tribune	EAA
Decreasing Powerlessness Through Communication: Black	Bacon, Mary M.	2/88	California Association	AAL
Dialect and Reading: Toward Redefining the Issues	Sims, Rudine	1982	Langer, J and E eds.	
Dialect and Reading: Toward Redefining the Issues Reader	Sims, Rudine	1982	Newark, DL Intern	AAAC
Difference vs. Disorder	American Speech			AALC

TITLE	AUTHOR	DATE	SOURCE	CATEGORY
Do We Have the Will to Educate All Children?	Hilliard, Asa III	9/91	Educational Leadership	ME
Does Phoneme Awareness Training in Kindergarten Make A Difference	Ball, Eileen.W	1991	Reading Research	AALC
Dropout Rate Cut to 18.2% Statewide	Merl, Jean	June 1992	Los Angeles Times	DR
Ebonics: My Unknown First Language	Cheketchsha, Malke		Communique, Nationa	AAL
Educating Poor Minority Children	Comer, James P.		Scientific America	EM
Education That Works: An Action Plan For the Education Of				EM
Essays, Calculators Added To New SAT's	Ordovensky, Pat	11/1/90	USA Today	T
Euclid Gifted/High Ability Bilingual Magnet School, The	Steintz, Victoria			
Expanding Students' Potential Through Family Literacy	Nuckolls, Maryann	9/91	Educational Leadership	P
Experts Say Practice Makes Students Good Readers	Quan, Elaine	2/22/91	United Teachers	L
Exploring Multi-Ethnic Literature for Children	Williams, Sharon			AAC
Fads Won't Help Black Kids Excel	Rowan, Carl T.,	4/5/91	Chicago Sun Times	EAA
Getting Smart: The Social Construction of Intellegence	Howard, Jeffery	1/30/90	The Efficacy Instit	EM
How Schools Perpetuate Illiteracy	LaVergne	9/91	Educational Leadership	EM
How the U.S. Failed in Science	Roark, Anne C.	11/8/90	Los Angeles Times	MS
Hundred Amazing Facts About the Negro With Complete Proof	Rogers, J. A.	1957	Futuro Press, Inc.	H
In Oakland, A Textbook Case of Trouble	Trombley, William	11-4-91	Los Angeles Times	SS
Increasing Parental Involvement In Elementary Schools	Galen, Harlene	1/91	Young Children	PR
Interlanguage	Selinker, Larry			BE

TITLE	AUTHOR	DATE	SOURCE	CATEGORY
Introduction: Language and the Teaching Learnng Process			Scott, Jerrie Cobb	
Investigation of Transfer in Second Language Phonology	Broselow, Ellen			BE
Is Literacy Possible for All Our Students?	Quan, Elaine	1/25/91	United Teachers	L
Language Acquisition Theory Revolutionizing Instruction		4/1/87	Education Week	BE
Language Diversity and Learning	Delpit, Lisa D.	1990	Perspectives on Talk	AAL
Language Differences: Dialects and Bilingualism				BE
Learning to Read: The Never-Ending Debate	Smith, Frank	February	Phi Delta Kappan	R
Legacies and Lessons from Independent Schools	Johnson, Sylvia	Spring 199	The Journal of Negro	AAL
Making It and Going Home The Attitudes of Black People	Cazden, Courtney		National Association	AAL
Maryland Standard English Program for Blacks Stir Contro	Armstrong, Liz		Washington Newspaper	
Math, Verbal SAT Scores Fall in US States	Gordon, Larry	8/27/91	Los Angeles Times	T
Model for Collaborative Service Delivery for Students With	Committee of Lan		American Speech	BE
More Seniors Pass College Exams	Merl, Jean	5/2/91	Los Angeles Times	T
Multicultural Curriculum Worthy of Our Multicultural Society	Editors of American	Winter 199	American Educator	ME
Native Language Instruction	Gonzales, Teresa			BE
Native Language Instruction Found to Aid LEP Students	Miller Julie	10/31/90	Education Week	BE
News: Negative Focus Districts		12/11/90	Los Angeles Times	D

TITLE	AUTHOR	DATE	SOURCE	CATEGORY
The Picture of Population	Coley, Joan Develin	April 1990	Journal of Reading	R
Overcoming Learned Helplessness in At-Risk Readers				
Pedagogical Problems of Using Second Language Techniques	Johnsons, Kenneth	1969	University of Illinios	AAL
Phonetic Transfer and the Teaching of Pronunciation	Catford, J.C.			AALC
Portland Parents Boycott Schools Over Education of Minorities	Viadero, Debra	2/13/91	Education Week	EAA
Portrait of Reuven Feuerstein	Goldberg, Mark F.	9/91	Educational Leadership	AAL
Position of the American Speech Language Hearing Association				
Power to the Parents!	Alibrandi, Joseph and Burnstein, Nancy	March 2,	Los Angeles Times	P
Preparing Teachers to Work with Culturally Diverse Students		9/10/'89	Journal of Teacher	M
Program and Organization Models I & II			LAUSD Master Plan	BE
Promoting the Success of Latino Langauge Minority Students	Cucas, Tamera	8/90	Harvard Education	BE
Public Document of the California State Board of Public Institutions		4/85	English Today	BE
Put Performance Exams to the Test	Kelly Dennis	11/1/90	USA Today	T
Radical Changes	Benjamin, Playth	4/20/91	Emerge	AAP
Report: Diversity Training For Teacher's Scare		1/21/91	EDCAL	M
Research for Bilingual Education, The	Rossell, Cristin	WIN/90	Equity and Choice	BE
Richmond School Tax Facing Tough Vote	Hallissy, Erin	April 10,	San Francisco Chronicle	
Schools Are Not Families		3/4/91	New York Times	
Self-Assessment of Second Language Ability: The Role of Respect	Heilenman, L. Kat	1990		EAA

TITLE	AUTHOR	DATE	SOURCE	CATEGORY
Social Dialects	Committee on the	9/83	American Speech	BE
Sorting Out the Self-Esteem Controversy	Beane, James A.	9/91	Educational Leadership	EAA
Staff Development for Desegregated School	Sleeter, Christine	9/90	Phi Delta Kappan	M
Superintendent's Symposium Program Unveiled 1991 Theme		11/19/90	EDCAL	L
Teacher Empowerment: The Key to Student Literacy	Quan, Elaine	3/8/91	United Teachers	CT
Teachers Serve Fresh "Hots" Lessons at Thinking Table	Walters, Laurel	11/16/90	Los Angeles Times	SE
The Affirmation of Self	Morris, Jimmy O	8/9/90		AAL
The Black Child: Language and Communication	Wilson, Amos. N	1987	The Developmental	AAL
The Black English Controversy and Its Implication	Starks, Judith A		Black English, EDU	EAA
The Bus Don't Stop Here	Allis, Sam	12/17/90	Times	EAA
The Chauvinism We Hate Isn't Our Path, Either: Afrocentrism	Njeri, Itabari T		Los Angeles Times	ME
The Children Can No Longer Wait an Action Plan to End Low		1990		
The Disuniting of America: What We Stand to Lose If Multicultural Education	Schlesinger, Arthur		American Educator	PR
The Good and the Bad the Difference	Kantrowitz, Bar		Newsweek	AAL
The Historical Development of Ebonics: An Examination	Smith, Ernie, PH. D	1977	Paper No. 38	BE
The Language Gap	Quintanilla, Mich	6/9/91	Los Angeles Times	AAL
The Quality School Curriculum	Glasser, William	May 1992	Phi Delta Kappa	
The Silenced Dialogue: Power and Pedagogy in Educating Other People	Delpit, Lisa D.		Harvard Educational	
Think-Pair-Share, Thinktrix, Thinklinks, and Weird Facts	Lyman, Frank T. Jr.		Enhancing Thinking	CT and CG

TITLE	AUTHOR	DATE	SOURCE	CATEGORY
Today's America Needs Many Tongues	Fairchild, Halford		Los Angeles Times	BE
Toward an Inarticulate and Aliterate Society			Endangered Minds	L
Turned on to Reading and Writing		May/June 1/91	Electronic Learning	S
Understanding Bilingual and Bicultural Young Children	Soto, Lourdes Dia		BE	
Unearthing Egypt's "Pyramid City"	Maugh, Thomas	7/22/91	Los Angeles Times	H
Using Standardized Achievement and Oral Proficiency Tests	Patrick, Blanche		University of Texas	SLAA
What is a Community?: A Principal's View of James Comer's School	Shipley, Diana	Spring 199	Equity and Choice, Vo	

English For Your Success:
Strategies Handbook

Research Articles and Periodicals

A Pocket for Corduroy. Freeman, Don. 1978. Scholastic. $2.21-$4.95. ISBN 0-590-31970-1. **Fiction**

Andrew Young Freedom Fighter. Roberts, Naurice. 1983. Regensteiner Publishing Enterp. ISBN 0-516-03450-2. **Biography**

Barbara Jordan. Roberts, Naurice. 1990. Children's Press. ISBN 0-516-03511-8. **Biography**

Black Scientist of America. Donovan, Richard X. 1990. National Book Company. ISBN 0-89420-265-0. $8.95. **Biographical Activity**

Children of Long Ago. Little, Lessie.1988. Philomel Books. ISBN 0-399-21473-9.

Desmond Tutu. Green Carol. 1986. Children's Press. ISBN 0-516-03634-3. **Biography**

Ella Baker. 1989. Silver Burdett Press. $7.95. **Biography**

Franklin in the Dark. Bourgeois, Paulette. 1986. Scholastic. ISBN 0-590-44506-5. $2.21-$4.95. **Fiction**

Frederick Douglass. McKissack, Pat & Fre. 1989. Children's Press. ISBN 0-516-03221-6. **Biography**

Galimoto. Williams, Karen. 1990. Lothrop, Lee and Shepard Books. ISBN 0-688-087890. $13.95.

Harold Washington. Roberts, Naurice. 1988. Children's Press. ISBN 0-516-03657-2. **Biography**

Hidden Animals. Drew, David. 1988. Rigby. ISBN 0-7312-1013-1. **Science Big Book**

Honey I Love. Greenfield, Eloise. 1986. Harper and Row Jr. Books. ISBN 0-06-443097-9. $3.95. **Poetry**

I Am Eyes Ni Macho. Ward, Leila. 1978. Scholastic. ISBN 0-590-40990-5. $3.95. **Fiction**

Jackie Robinson. Greene, Carol. 1990. Children's Press. ISBN 0-516-04211-4. **Biography**

Jamaica's Find. Havill, Juanita. 1986. Scholastic. ISBN 0-590-65708-9. $2.21-$4.95. **Fiction**

Jamberry. Degen, Bruce. 1989. Scholastic. ISBN 0-590-44156-6. $2.21-$4.95. **Rhyming Tale**

James Weldon Johnson. McKissack, Pat & Fre. 1990. Children's Press. ISBN 0-516-04174-6. **Biograph**y

Jessie Jackson. Young, Andrew. 1990. Silver Burdett Press. ISBN 0-382-24064. $7.95. **Biography**

Leontyne Price. Williams, Sylvia. 19184. Children's Press. ISBN 0-516-03531-2. **Biography**

Lord of the Dance. Tadjo, Veronica. 1989. Lippincott. ISBN 0-397-32351-1. $12.95. **African Folktale**

Martin Luther King. McKissack, Pat. 1989. Children's Press. ISBN 0-516-03206-2. **Biography**

Martin Luther King Jr.. Greene, Carol. 1989. Children's Press. ISBN 0-516-04205-X. **Biography**

Mary McLeod Bethune. McKissack, Pat. 1989. Children's Press. ISBN 0-516-03218-6. **Biography**

Mufaro's Beautiful Daughters. Steptoe, John. 1987. Lothrop, Lee and Sheppard. ISBN 0-688-04045-4. **African Folktale**

Nathaniel Talking. Greenfield, Eloise. 1988. Black Butterfly Children's Book. ISBN 0-86316-200-2. **Poetry**

Nelson Mandela. McKissack, Pat & Fre. 1989. Children's Press. ISBN 0-516003266-6. **Biography**

Noisy Nora. Wells, Rosemary. 1973. Scholastic. ISBN 0-590-28315-4. $2.21-$4.95. **Fiction**

Paul Lawrence Dunbar. McKissack, Pat. 1989. Children's Press. ISBN 0-516-03218-6. **Biography**

Rosa Parks. Young, Andrew. 1990. Silver Burdett Press. ISBN 0-382-24065-0. $7.95. **Biography**

Stokely Carmichael. Young, Andrew. 1990. Silver Burdett Press. IBSN 0-382-24056-1. $7.95. **Biography**

Tadpole Diary. Drew, David. 1988. Rigby. IBSN 0-9473-2852-1. **Science Big Book**

Ten, Nine, Eight. Bang, Molly. 1983. Scholastic. IBSN 0-590-42663-X. $2.21-$4.95. **Counting Book**

The Life of the Butterfly. Drew, David. 1988. Rigby. IBSN 0-7327-0131-4. **Science Big Book**

The Talking Eggs. San Souci, Robert. 1989. Scholastic. IBSN 0-590-44189-2. $2.96. **African American**

Thurgood Marshall. Hargrove, Jim. 1989. Silver Burdett. IBSN 0-382-24058-8. $7.95. **Biography**

Two Ways to Count to Ten. Dee, Ruby. 1988. Henry Holt and Co..IBSN 0-8050-0407-6. $12.95. **African Folktale**

Ty's One-man Band. Walker, Mildred Pitts. 1980. Scholastic. IBSN 0-590-40178-5. $2.96-$4.95. **Fiction**

Village of Round and Square Houses. Grifalconi, Ann. 1990. Little Brown and Co.ISBN 0-316-32862-6. $14.95. **African Folktale**

What Mary Jo Shared. Udry, Janice May. 1966. Scholastic. IBSN 0-590-65710-0. $1.69-$4.95. **Fiction**

COMPUTER PROGRAMS AND VIDEO LISTINGS
CODES AND CATEGORIES

ABBREVIATED CODE	REFERENCE CATEGORY
AAL	AFRICAN AMERICAN LANGUAGE
AAM	AFRICAN AMERICAN MALES
BE	BILINGUAL EDUCATION
C	CULTURE
CT	CRITICAL THINKING
D	DEMOGRAPHICS
DR	DROP-OUT RATE
E	EDUCATION
EAA	EDUCATION & THE AFRICAN AMERICAN
EM	EDUCATING MINORITIES
H	HISTORY
L	LITERATURE
LA	LANGUAGE ACQUISITION/DEVELOPMENT
MAE	MAINSTREAM AMERICAN ENGLISH
MS	MATH AND SCIENCE
NC	NON-CIRCULATING
P	PARENT RESOURCE
R	REFERENCE
RD	READING
SLA	SECOND LANGUAGE ACQUISITION
T	TEACHER RESOURCE
TA	THEMATIC APPROACH
TE	TESTING
W	WHOLE LANGUAGE
WR	WRITING

COMPUTER PROGRAM AND VIDEO LISTING

TITLE	AUTHOR	CATEGORY
Apple Learning Series	Early Language	LA
Collaborative Teaching	LeMoine, Noma	T
Developing Positive Self-Images & Discipline in Black Children	Kunjufu, Jawanza	P-AAM-T
Dissemination of Elementary Course Of Study	L.A.U.S.D.	E
Free Your Mind Return to the Source: African Origins	Hilliard, ASA G.	H
From African American Language to Mainstream American English	Rollins, Jean	AAL
Literacy 2000 Overview	Davidson, Avelyn	V
Master Keys to Ancient Kemet (Egypt) and Listervelt Middleton	Hilliard Asa. G.	H
Parents as Partners in Reading: A Family Literacy Training Program	Edwards, Patricia, Ph.D.	RD-T
Reading Symposium	Teale, William, Dr.	RD-T
Roots: Elementary Students and Roots	Kunjufu, Jawanza	H
Giving the Gift of Reading Separate But Equal-Part II	Scholastic	RD
Something to Say in a Different Way		LA
The African American Holiday of Kwanzaa	Bahati, Rashid *Producer*	C
The Story of English: A Muse of Fire Program	MacNeil, Robert,*Narrator* & The Guid Scot	MAE
The Story of English English Speaking World: Program 1	MacNeil, Robert	MAE
The Story of English: Black on White Program 5 Pioneers	MacNeil, Robert, *Narrator*	AAL-MAE
The Story of English: A Look Into the Future	MacNeil, Robert, *Narrator*	MAE
The Story of English: MAE The Muvver Tongue Program 7	MacNeil, Robert, *Narrator*	MAE
Tony Brown's Journal	Brown, Tony & Winnie Mandela	H-C
Women of South Africa Program 2	Compiled by R. Degraffinreid	C-H

additive approach

Teaches mainstream English as a second language to speakers of African American Language. It incorporates second-language methodology and emphasizes communication through content. Provides staff development for educators and paraprofessional that imparts knowledge of AAL as a viable language with its own system of rules, sounds, and meaning and includes information on the culture and learning styles of African American students. Identifies and builds on the learning styles and strengths of African American students to develop instructional strategies that foster academic success. Children continue to speak their primary language even after mastering a new language

affective filters

Feelings such as anxiety, lack of confidence, poor self-esteem, and inadequate motivation that can block the learning process. To the greatest practical extent, teachers must take steps to minimize these filters.

African American Language

The natural home language spoken by most African Americans. It's underlying structure (including syntax) is rooted in the Bantu languages spoken by Africans residing in a wide area covering parts of Central and Western Africa (i.e., the Niger-Congo). However, the language uses the vocabulary of Mainstream American English.

Bantu

A related group of African languages spoken by inhabitants of the Niger-Congo region of Africa (includes areas of Central and Western Africa).

contrastive analysis

Consists of comparing and contrasting the linguistic features (phonology, morphology, syntax, lexicon, semantics, and discourse patterns) of the primary language and the target language. As an instructional strategy, contrastive analysis is a natural extension of literature that feature the students' primary language and MAE. For example, in the African American literature title *Flossie and the Fox* by Patricia McKissack, Flossie, the main character in the story, says, "I ain't never seen a fox before." A possible MAE translation might be, "I haven't ever seen a fox before." In this example, constrastive analysis focuses student attention on a distinctive feature of AAmericanL--multiple negation (aine and never used concurrently). Samples of students' daily oral and written language may also be used for contrastive analysis.

cooperative grouping (cooperative learning)

Using small, heterogeneous groups to facilitate learning. For example, small group activities may be used to encourage language development and the sharing of ideas and learning strategies. Students are encouraged to communicate during group projects and activities. Students rotate through various roles as editors, typists, readers, speakers, etc., to ensure equal participation.

creole

A language which was *pidgin* at an earlier historical stage, but which became the principal language of a speech community. One of the best known creoles is Haitian (French) Creole.

creolist

A linguist who specializes in the study of creole languages. The creolist theory holds that the home language spoken by many African Americans today derives from a "pidgin" or trade language that white slavers and Africans developed during the African slave trade.

deficit theory

Holds that the language spoken by most African Americans is an inferior dialect of MAE which resulted from cognitive deficiencies and from anatomical and psychological deviations in the speech mechanism.

Ebonics

Derived from the terms ebony (black) and phonics (sound) and refers to "the linguistic . . . features which . . . represent the communicative competence of the West African, Caribbean, and United States slave descendants of African origin. It includes the various idioms, patois, argots, ideolects, and social dialects of black people."

education technology

Generally refers to electronic equipment or approaches that can be used to facilitate instruction. Equipment includes, for example, desktop computers and related peripherals and software, television, VCR, spell checkers and electronic thesauruses, calculators. Distance learning is an example of an education technology that that can facilitate instruction.

ethnolinguist theory

Holds that the home language spoken by most African Americans today adopts the lexicon or vocabulary of MAE but shares the deep structure of Bantu languages spoken in the Niger-Congo region of Central and Western Africa.

language acquisition

The process of learning to speak like the adults of a given community; occurs between the ages of two and five.

language-experience approach

A meaning-centered approach to language learning and literacy development that guides students through a language experience that results in their producing reading material based on their own ideas and interests. The students recall experiences, recount stories, or describe works of art that they have created while the teacher writes their words verbatim. Students are encouraged to say what they have heard or experienced, read what was said, and then write what was read. An underlying assumption of this approach is that all students can say what they think, read what they say, and write what they read. The language-experience approach has been used successfully with primary-age children showing emergent literacy skills and with students acquiring English as a second language.

Mainstream American English

The written and oral language employed by American entities accepted as standard. Written MAE is reflected in standard American textbooks, encyclopedias, major newspapers, journals, etc. Oral MAE is practiced, for example, by television and radio newscasters, college professors, and teachers. Oral MAE may vary regionally (for example, Southern MAE or New England MAE).

multiple modality teaching

To infuse instruction continually with multimedia resources, instructional television, visual stimuli, and other modes of instruction. The teacher allows students to physically participate in activities, including lots of hands-on science and math activities and investigations. Teachers use a variety of modes (auditory, visual, kinesthetic, tactile, etc.) to present each lesson and activity. Teachers facilitate student production of multimedia reports, visual displays, etc.

Niger-Congo

A region of Central and Western Africa from which most enslaved Africans originated.

parental component

Provides educational experiences, resources and support to parents in an effort to increase their knowledge of A AL, history and culture and to enhance their skill in providing empowering support to their children.

personal thesaurus

Students' personal list of word concepts that is developed while participating in *LDPAAS*. The list emphasizes synonyms, antonyms, prefixes, and suffixes that center on students' own experiences, whether culled from literature or real authentic events from the students' lives. Words are examined in context. Dictionaries are used to verify or support student-generated word meanings. The expectation is that the expanded vocabulary will reappear in students' oral and written productions and become an active part of their vocabulary.

pidgin

A language which has no native speakers. It dispenses features speakers from a great variety of languages would find odd or difficult to learn.

receptive language

The language that an individual learns through hearing, including what teachers and parents read, what is heard on television, the radio, and other audio media.

sheltered instruction/specially designed academic instruction in English (SDAIE)

A method of instruction using MAE that utilizes language-sensitive techniques to provide comprehensible input in a manner that lowers the affective filter for language-different students. It includes: (1) a simplified, slower rate of speech, (2) controlled vocabulary, (3) repetition, (4) using gestures and facial expressions, and (5) using visuals, props, and models. The teacher focuses on meaning and the message that students communicate. Therefore, correction is minimal and occurs only in a restatement form. For example, an African American student tells the teacher, "I ain't got no glue stick." The teacher might respond, "No, you don't have a glue stick. I'll get one for you."

teachable moments

The identification and comparison of the differences between MAE and AAL are generally limited to the language arts period. However, a typical school day offers many opportunities for teachers to implement second-language instruction. Contrastive analysis, for example, could be employed within the context of a content lesson to reinforce the concepts being taught/learned. Teachable moments can also be created, for example, by inserting language breaks throughout the instructional day.

whole language approach

An approach to language instruction based on the premise that students acquire literacy through meaningful, comprehensible input. The whole-language approach surrounds students with language from which they construct meaning. It integrates listening, speaking, reading, and writing into a "whole" language experience. This speech-to-print process promotes learning of language skills in context while focusing on meaning. Whole-language strategies often rely on literature-based instruction as a basis for student encounters with meaningful text.

[1] See Dillard, p.300.
[2] From Williams, p.vi.
[3] See Dillard, p.302.
[4] See Dillard, p.303.

Alleyne, M. (1971). "Linguistic continuity of Africa in the Caribbean." In J. H. Richards (ed.), *Topics in Afro-American Studies*. New York, NY: Black Academy Press.

Bailey, B.L. (1966). *Jamaican Creole Syntax*. London: Cambridge University Press.

Baratz, J. "Teaching reading in an urban Negro school system." In F. Williams (ed.), *Language and Poverty*. Illinois: Markham.

Baugh, John (1983). *Black Street Speech*. Texas: University of Texas Press.

Bereiter, C. , and Englemann, S. (1966). *Teaching Disadvantaged Children in the preschool*. New Jersey: Prentice-Hall.

Bernstein, B. (1951). "Social Class and Linguistic Development: A theory of social Learning." In A. H. Hakey, J. Fland, & C.A. Anderson (eds.), *Education, Economy, and Society*. New York: Free Press.

Chambers, J. W. (Ed.) (1983). *Black English, Educational Equity, and the Law*. Ann Arbor: Karoma Publishers, Inc.

Cran, W. (producer and director) (1986). *The story of English: Black on White* (Program 5) [Video].

Cummins, J. (1989). *Empowering Minority Students*. Sacramento: California Association for Bilingual Education.

Dandy, E. B. (1991). *Black Communications: Breaking Down the Barriers*. Chicago: African American Images.

Dillard, J. L. (1972). *Black English: Its History and Usage in the United States*. New York, NY: Random House.

Fairchild, H. & Edwards-Evans, S. (1990). "African American Dialects and Schooling: A Review." *Journal of Black Psychology*, 20.

Fasold, R. W. and Shuy, R. W. (1970). *Teaching Standard English in the Inner City*. Washington, D.C.: Center for Applied Linguistics.

Ferdman, B. M. (1990). "Literacy and Cultural Identity". *Harvard Educational Review*, 60, 181-204.

Hale-Benson, J. E. (1986). *Black children: Their Roots, Culture and Learning Styles*. Baltimore: The John Hopkins University Press.

Harber, J. R., & Bryen, D. N. (1976). "Black English and the Task of Reading." *Review of Educational Research*, 46, 387-405.

Hoover, M. R. (1979). "A Semiforeign Language Approach to Teaching Reading to Bidialectal Children." In Shafer & Newark (eds.), *Applied linguistics and reading*, International Reading Association, 63-71.

Jackson, K. (1996). *America Is Me*. New York: HarperCollins.

Labov, W. (1970). *The Study of Nonstandard English*. Champaign, Ill.: National Council of Teachers of English.

Labov, W. (1983). "Recognizing Black English in the classroom." In J. W. Chambers (ed.), *Black English: Educational equity and the law*. Ann Arbor, Michigan: Karoma Publishers, Inc.

Ladefoged, P. (1964). *A Phonetic study of West African languages*.

Ladson Billings, G. (1992). "Liberatory consequences of literacy: A case of culturally relevant instruction for African American students." *Journal of Negro Education*, 61, 378-391.

Larkin, J. M. (1993). "Rethinking basic skills Instruction with Urban Students." *The Educational Forum*, 57, 412-419.

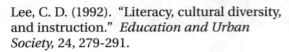

Lee, C. D. (1992). "Literacy, cultural diversity, and instruction." *Education and Urban Society*, 24, 279-291.

Martin Luther King Junior Elementary School Children, et al. v Ann Arbor School District Board (July 1979). Civil Action No. 7-71861, US District Court.

Ogbu, J. U. (1992). "Understanding Cultural Diversity and Learning." *Educational Researcher*, 21, 5-14.

Shade, B. J. (1982). "Afro-American Cognitive Style: A Variable in School success?" *Review of Educational Research*, 52, 219-244.

Smith, E. A. (1977). *The historical development of ebonics: An Examination and analysis of three linguistic views and ideological perspectives*, 1-15, California State University, Fullerton.

Smith, E. A. (1992), African American Language Behavior: A World of Difference. In P. H. Dreyer (ed.), *Reading the world: Multimedia and multicultural learning in today's classrooms,* Claremont Graduate School Conference.

Smitherman, G. (1977). *Talkin and testifyin: The language of Black America.* Boston: Houghton Mifflin.

Spache, G. (1975). *Good Reading for the Disadvantaged Reader.* Champaign, Illinois: Garrard.

Stewart, W. (1967). "Sociolinguistic Factors in the History of American Negro Dialect." *Florida Foreign Language Reporter*, Spring.

Stewart, W. (1968). "Continuity and Change in American Negro Dialects." *Florida Foreign Language Reporter,* Spring.

Turner, L. D. (1949). *Africanisms in the Gullah Dialect.* Ann Arbor: The University of Michigan Press.

Welmers, W. (1973). *African language structures.*

Williams, Robert L., Ed. (1970). *Ebonics: The True Language of Black folks.* The Institute of Black Studies, St. Louis.

Williams, Ronald and Wolfram, Walt (1982). *A Linguistic Description of Social Dialects, part II.* University of the District of Columbia and the Center for Applied Linguistics.

Wilson, Amos N. (1978/1987), *The Developmental Psychology of the Black child.* New York, N.Y.: African Research Publication

Weddington, Gloria Tolliver, Ed. (1979). "Ebonics (Black English): Implications for Education." *Journal of Black Studies*, 9:4.

Wolfram, W. A. (1969). *A Sociolinguistic Description of Detroit Negro Speech.* Arlington: Center for Applied Linguistics.

Woodson, Carter G. (1990). *The mis-education of the Negro.* New Jersey : Africa World Press, Inc.,.